The Walker & Mason
Medieval Hot Chocolate Mix
Recipe Journal

ISBN Paperback
978-1-989647-28-8

A Byrd Press Publication
Toronto
www.byrdpress.com
publisher@byrdpress.com

cover design R.H. Mason
interior art Felipe Silva

for Walker

Table of Contents

Introduction

Hot Chocolate Mix: Breakfast

Hot Chocolate Mix: Desserts

1. Cinnamon and Nutmeg Spiced Hot Chocolate Creme Brulee...21

2. Cinnamon and Nutmeg Spiced Hot Chocolate Scones with Clotted Cream...22

3. Cinnamon and Sugar Dusted Medieval Hot Chocolate Donuts...23

4. Cinnamon and Nutmeg Spiced Medieval Hot Chocolate Cheesecake...25

5. Medieval Hot Chocolate Flavored Bread and Butter Pudding with Raisins...27

6. Medieval Hot Chocolate Flavored Churros with Cinnamon Sugar...28

7. Medieval Hot Chocolate Flavored Chocolate Chip Cookies with Sea Salt...30

8. Medieval Hot Chocolate Flavored Panna Cotta with Dark Chocolate Shavings...33

9. Medieval Hot Chocolate Flavored Tiramisu with Cocoa and Mascarpone...35

10. Medieval Hot Chocolate Flavored Yogurt Parfait with Granola and Honey...36

11. Medieval Hot Chocolate Infused Chocolate Bark with Almonds and Sea Salt...37

12. Medieval Hot Chocolate Infused Chocolate Truffles with Cocoa Powder...38

13. Medieval Hot Chocolate Infused Pecan Pie with Whipped Cream...40

14. Medieval Hot Chocolate Infused Waffles with Fresh Berries and Cream...41

15. Spiced Hot Chocolate Chia Seed Pudding with Coconut Flakes...43

16. Spiced Hot Chocolate Mug Cake with Vanilla Ice Cream...44

17. Warm Medieval Hot Chocolate Bread Pudding with Vanilla Sauce...46

18. Warm Medieval Hot Chocolate Custard with Caramelized Sugar Topping...48

19. Warm Medieval Hot Chocolate Pudding with Whipped Cream...50

20. Warm Medieval Hot Chocolate Rice Pudding with Raisins and Cinnamon...51

21. Warm Medieval Hot Chocolate Tarts with Raspberry Jam...52

22. Medieval Hot Chocolate Scented Caramel Apples with Toppings..56

Hot Chocolate Mix: Energy Bars and Balls

1. Spiced Hot Chocolate Energy Bites with Oats and Almond Butter...57

2. Spiced Hot Chocolate Energy Bars with Nuts and Dried Fruit..58

3. Spiced Hot Chocolate Energy Bars with Quinoa and Avocado...59

4. Spiced Hot Chocolate Energy Balls with Chickpeas and Dates...61

Spicy Hot Chocolate Mix: Breakfast

1. Cinnamon and Long Pepper Spiced Hot Chocolate French Toast with Berries...65

2. Cinnamon and Long Pepper Spiced Hot Chocolate Smoothie with Banana and Almond Milk...66

3. Cinnamon and Long Pepper Spiced Hot Chocolate Waffles with Berries and Whipped Cream..67

4. Long Pepper and Clove Spiced Hot Chocolate Pancakes with Maple Syrup...68

5. Long Pepper and Nutmeg Spiced Hot Chocolate Pancake Stack with Spiced Syrup...69

6. Spicy Medieval Hot Chocolate Scented Oatmeal with Brown Sugar, Nuts, and Avocado..71

Spicy Hot Chocolate Mix: Desserts

1. Cinnamon and Clove Spiced Hot Chocolate Mousse with Whipped Cream...73

2. Cinnamon and Clove Spiced Hot Chocolate Muffins with a Cocoa Drizzle...74

3. Cinnamon and Long Pepper Spiced Hot Chocolate Cheesecake with Chocolate Ganache...76

4. Cinnamon and Long Pepper Spiced Hot Chocolate Donuts with Sugar Glaze...78

5. Cinnamon and Long Pepper Spiced Hot Chocolate French Toast Roll-Ups with Homemade Hazelnut Spread..80

6. Long Pepper and Cinnamon Spiced Hot Chocolate Brownies...82

Fare Well...126

Time's Fare...127

Recipes for the Chocolate Mixes...129

Welcome to "The Walker& Mason Medieval Hot Chocolate Mix Recipe Journal" - a very small cookbook that invites you on a journey through time, where the rich and aromatic flavors of the medieval era come to life in a modern culinary experience. Delve into a collection of decadent recipes inspired by the opulent feasts and banquets of the past, each crafted using the exquisite 'Medieval Hot Chocolate Mix.' Discover an array of delightful and indulgent dishes that evoke a sense of nostalgia and comfort, while celebrating the rich history and cultural heritage of the medieval period. From luscious desserts to savory delights, this cookbook offers a delightful fusion of traditional flavors and contemporary culinary techniques, providing a truly unique and memorable dining experience for all. Embark on a culinary adventure and savor the timeless allure of the medieval era with every delectable bite.

About Chocolate in the Middle Ages

Between the 9th and 15th centuries in Europe, there is no direct evidence of chocolate consumption as we know it today. Chocolate, in the form of cacao beans, was primarily cultivated and consumed by the Mesoamerican civilizations such as the Mayans and Aztecs during this period. The use of chocolate was primarily confined to the regions where cacao was grown, and it was consumed in the form of a bitter, frothy beverage, often mixed with spices, chili, and other natural flavorings.

The consumption of chocolate in Europe became prominent only after the Spanish conquest of the Aztec Empire in the early 16th century, led by Hernán Cortés. It was during this time that cacao and the Aztec chocolate beverage known as "xocolātl" were introduced to the Spanish court. The Spanish explorers and colonizers were fascinated by this exotic beverage, and it eventually made its way to Spain, where it gained popularity among the aristocracy and clergy.

In its early introduction to Europe, chocolate was consumed primarily as a beverage. The original Mesoamerican recipe for the chocolate drink included ground roasted cacao beans mixed with water and various spices, such as chili, vanilla, and achiote, creating a rich, frothy, and bitter beverage that was often served during religious ceremonies and as a symbol of wealth and luxury among the Aztec and Mayan elites.

The adoption of chocolate in Europe during the 16th century led to the development of various adaptations and modifications to the original Mesoamerican recipe. The addition of sugar and spices, such as cinnamon and other flavorings, transformed the bitter beverage into a sweeter and more palatable drink, setting the stage for the eventual evolution of chocolate into the various confectionery and culinary forms that we recognize and enjoy today.

RECIPES FOR MEDIEVAL CHOCOLATE MIX

Cinnamon and Nutmeg Spiced Hot Chocolate Cupcakes with Marshmallow Frosting

These Cinnamon and Nutmeg Spiced Hot Chocolate Cupcakes with Marshmallow Frosting are a delightful twist on a classic treat. The cupcakes are infused with a homemade hot chocolate mix, featuring warm spices like cinnamon, nutmeg, and a hint of cloves. Topped with a fluffy marshmallow frosting, these cupcakes offer a perfect balance of rich flavors and comforting sweetness. Enjoy them as a cozy dessert or a special treat for any occasion.

For the Cupcakes:

Ingredients:

- 1 and 1/2 cups all-purpose flour
- 1 teaspoon baking powder
- 1/2 teaspoon baking soda
- 1/4 teaspoon salt
- 1/2 cup unsalted butter, softened
- 1 cup Medieval Hot Chocolate Mix
- 2 large eggs
- 1 teaspoon vanilla extract
- 1/2 cup milk
- 1/2 cup hot water

Instructions:

1. Preheat your oven to 350°F (175°C). Line a cupcake pan with liners.
2. In a medium bowl, whisk together the flour, baking powder, baking soda, and salt. Set aside.
3. In a separate large mixing bowl, cream the butter and hot chocolate mix together until light and fluffy.

4. Add the eggs one at a time, mixing well after each addition. Stir in the vanilla extract.
5. Alternately add the dry ingredients and the milk to the batter, beginning and ending with the dry ingredients. Mix until just combined.
6. Stir in the hot water until the batter is smooth.
7. Divide the batter evenly among the cupcake liners, filling them about two-thirds of the way full.
8. Bake for 18-20 minutes, or until a toothpick inserted into the center of a cupcake comes out clean.
9. Allow the cupcakes to cool completely before frosting.

For the Marshmallow Frosting:

Ingredients:

- 1 cup unsalted butter, softened
- 3 cups confectioners' sugar
- 1 teaspoon vanilla extract
- 1/4 teaspoon salt
- 1 cup marshmallow fluff

Instructions:

1. In a large mixing bowl, beat the softened butter until creamy.
2. Gradually add the confectioners' sugar, vanilla extract, and salt, and continue to beat until well combined and smooth.
3. Gently fold in the marshmallow fluff until fully incorporated.
4. Pipe or spread the frosting onto the cooled cupcakes.
5. Optionally, sprinkle a pinch of cinnamon and nutmeg on top of each frosted cupcake for garnish.

Cinnamon and Nutmeg Spiced Hot Chocolate Overnight Oats with Chia Seeds

These Cinnamon and Nutmeg Spiced Hot Chocolate Overnight Oats with Chia Seeds make for a delicious and nutritious breakfast option, combining the comforting flavors of hot chocolate with the health benefits of oats and chia seeds. Enjoy the convenience of preparing this wholesome meal the night before for a hassle-free and satisfying morning.

Ingredients:

- 1/2 cup rolled oats
- 1 tablespoon chia seeds
- 2 tablespoons Medieval Hot Chocolate Mix
- 1/2 teaspoon ground cinnamon
- 1/4 teaspoon ground nutmeg
- 1 cup milk (dairy or plant-based)
- 1 tablespoon honey or maple syrup (optional, for added sweetness)
- Fresh berries or sliced bananas, for topping

Instructions:

1. In a mason jar or airtight container, combine the rolled oats, chia seeds, Medieval Hot Chocolate Mix, ground cinnamon, and ground nutmeg.
2. Pour in the milk and add honey or maple syrup if desired. Stir well to ensure all the ingredients are fully combined.
3. Cover the jar or container and refrigerate it overnight, or for at least 4-6 hours, allowing the oats and chia seeds to soak and soften.
4. Before serving, give the mixture a good stir to combine all the ingredients thoroughly.
5. Top the Cinnamon and Nutmeg Spiced Hot Chocolate Overnight Oats with a handful of fresh berries or sliced bananas for an added burst of flavor and texture.

Cinnamon and Nutmeg Spiced Medieval Hot Chocolate French Toast

The origins of French toast are believed to date back to ancient times, with variations of the dish appearing in cultures across the globe. While the exact origin is not entirely clear, many food historians suggest that the idea of soaking bread in a mixture of eggs and milk may have developed as a way to repurpose stale bread and prevent food waste.

The dish gained popularity during medieval times in Europe. It was often referred to as "pain perdu" in France, which translates to "lost bread," reflecting the practice of using up leftover or stale bread. The concept of dipping bread in a mixture of eggs and milk before frying it in butter or oil was a simple and effective way to transform old bread into a flavorful and satisfying meal.

French toast has evolved over the centuries and has been adapted in various cultures, each adding its own unique twist to the classic recipe. It has become a beloved breakfast dish around the world, enjoyed for its versatility and the ability to be customized with different toppings, spices, and flavorings.

Today, French toast remains a popular breakfast option in many countries, and its rich history reflects the ingenuity of utilizing simple ingredients to create a delicious and comforting dish enjoyed by people of all ages.

This Cinnamon and Nutmeg Spiced Medieval Hot Chocolate French Toast recipe offers a delightful twist on the classic breakfast dish, infusing it with the rich flavors of hot chocolate and warm spices reminiscent of the medieval era. Enjoy the comforting and aromatic blend of cinnamon and nutmeg combined with the

Ingredients:

- 4 slices of thick-cut bread (such as brioche or challah)
- 2 large eggs
- 1/2 cup milk
- 2 tablespoons Medieval Hot Chocolate Mix
- 1/2 teaspoon ground cinnamon
- 1/4 teaspoon ground nutmeg
- 1 teaspoon vanilla extract
- Butter or oil, for greasing the pan
- Maple syrup, powdered sugar, or fresh berries, for serving (optional)

Instructions:

1. In a shallow dish, whisk together the eggs, milk, Medieval Hot Chocolate Mix, ground cinnamon, ground nutmeg, and vanilla extract until well combined.
2. Dip each slice of bread into the mixture, allowing it to soak for a few seconds on each side.
3. In a skillet or griddle, melt a small amount of butter or heat a small amount of oil over medium heat.
4. Place the soaked bread slices in the skillet and cook for 2-3 minutes on each side, or until golden brown and cooked through.
5. Serve the Cinnamon and Nutmeg Spiced Medieval Hot Chocolate French Toast with a drizzle of maple syrup, a dusting of powdered sugar, or a handful of fresh berries, if desired.

Cinnamon and Nutmeg Spiced Hot Chocolate Pancakes with Maple Syrup and Berries

Enjoy the delightful and aromatic Cinnamon and Nutmeg Spiced Hot Chocolate Pancakes with Maple Syrup and Berries, where the rich and warm flavors of the Medieval Hot Chocolate Mix infuse the fluffy pancakes with a delightful richness, while the sweet and tangy berries and the luscious maple syrup add a burst of natural sweetness and a touch of indulgence. Savor these pancakes as a delightful breakfast option or as a charming treat to enjoy during a cozy brunch or special occasion.

Ingredients:

- 1 cup all-purpose flour
- 2 tablespoons Medieval Hot Chocolate Mix
- 2 teaspoons baking powder
- 1/4 teaspoon salt
- 1 cup milk
- 1 large egg
- 2 tablespoons melted butter
- 1 teaspoon vanilla extract
- 1/2 teaspoon ground cinnamon
- Fresh berries of your choice (such as strawberries, blueberries, or raspberries)
- Maple syrup, for serving

Instructions:

1. In a large mixing bowl, whisk together the all-purpose flour, Medieval Hot Chocolate Mix, baking powder, and salt.
2. In a separate bowl, whisk together the milk, egg,

melted butter, vanilla extract, and ground cinnamon until well combined.

3. Gradually pour the wet ingredients into the dry ingredients, stirring until just combined. Be careful not to overmix; a few lumps are okay.

4. Heat a non-stick skillet or griddle over medium heat and lightly grease it with butter or cooking spray.

5. Pour 1/4 cup of the pancake batter onto the skillet for each pancake. Cook until bubbles form on the surface, then flip and cook until the other side is golden brown.

6. Serve the Cinnamon and Nutmeg Spiced Hot Chocolate Pancakes with a generous drizzle of maple syrup and a handful of fresh berries on top.

§

Medieval Hot Chocolate Infused Rice Krispie Treats with Dark Chocolate Drizzle

Enjoy these delightful Krispie Treats with Dark Chocolate Drizzle, where the classic combination of crispy rice cereal and gooey marshmallows is elevated with the addition of rich and indulgent dark chocolate. These treats are perfect for enjoying as a delightful snack, a lunchbox treat, or a charming addition to any special occasion or gathering.

Ingredients:

- 3 tablespoons unsalted butter
- 1 package (10 ounces) marshmallows
- 6 cups crispy rice cereal
- 4 ounces dark chocolate, melted
- 2 tablespoons Medieval Hot Chocolate Mix

Instructions:

1. In a large saucepan, melt the butter over low heat. Add the marshmallows and stir until completely melted and smooth.
2. Remove the saucepan from the heat and quickly add the crispy rice cereal and the Medieval Hot Chocolate Mix. Stir until the cereal is evenly coated with the marshmallow mixture and the hot chocolate mix is well incorporated.
3. Transfer the mixture to a 9x13-inch baking dish and press it down firmly to create an even layer.
4. Drizzle the melted dark chocolate over the top of the treats, creating a decorative pattern.
5. Allow the treats to cool and the chocolate to set before cutting them into squares or bars.

§

Medieval Hot Chocolate Scented Cinnamon Rice Cakes with Fresh Fruit

Enjoy the delightful and aromatic Medieval Hot Chocolate Scented Cinnamon Rice Cakes with Fresh Fruit, where the warm and comforting notes of the hot chocolate mix infuse the delicate rice cakes with a delightful richness, while the fresh and vibrant fruits add a burst of natural sweetness and a touch of refreshing indulgence. Savor these rice cakes as a delightful breakfast option or as a delightful snack to enjoy at any time of the day.

Ingredients:

- 1 cup cooked white rice
- 1/4 cup Medieval Hot Chocolate Mix
- 1 teaspoon ground cinnamon

- 1 tablespoon honey or maple syrup
- Fresh fruits of your choice (such as sliced strawberries, blueberries, or raspberries)

- Optional toppings: additional honey or maple syrup, chopped nuts, or shredded coconut

Instructions:

1. In a mixing bowl, combine the cooked white rice, Medieval Hot Chocolate Mix, ground cinnamon, and honey or maple syrup. Mix well to ensure the flavors are evenly distributed.
2. Divide the rice mixture into portions and shape each portion into a round cake or patty.
3. Heat a non-stick skillet or griddle over medium heat and lightly grease it with oil or butter.
4. Place the rice cakes on the skillet and cook for 2-3 minutes on each side, or until they are lightly browned and heated through.
5. Remove the rice cakes from the skillet and arrange them on a serving plate.
6. Top the rice cakes with an assortment of fresh fruits and any optional toppings of your choice.
7. Drizzle additional honey or maple syrup over the rice cakes if desired.

§

Medieval Hot Chocolate Scented Oatmeal with Brown Sugar and Nuts

Enjoy the delightful and comforting flavors of the Medieval Hot Chocolate Scented Oatmeal with Brown Sugar and Nuts, where the rich and aromatic essence of the hot chocolate mix perfectly complements the wholesome texture of the oats and the delightful crunch of the nuts, creating a satisfying and nourishing breakfast option that is both indulgent and wholesome.

Ingredients:

- 1 cup old-fashioned rolled oats
- 2 cups water
- 1/2 cup Medieval Hot Chocolate Mix (1 cup cocoa powder, 1 cup granulated sugar, 1 teaspoon ground cinnamon, 1/2 teaspoon ground nutmeg, 1/4 teaspoon ground cloves, pinch of salt)
- 1/4 cup chopped nuts (such as almonds, walnuts, or pecans)
- 2 tablespoons brown sugar
- A pinch of salt

Instructions:

1. In a saucepan, bring the water to a boil. Stir in the rolled oats, Medieval Hot Chocolate Mix, and a pinch of salt.
2. Reduce the heat to medium-low and simmer the oatmeal, stirring occasionally, for 5-7 minutes, or until the oats are cooked and the mixture has thickened to your desired consistency.
3. Remove the oatmeal from the heat and stir in the brown sugar until it is fully dissolved.
4. Serve the Medieval Hot Chocolate Scented Oatmeal in bowls, garnishing each portion with a sprinkle of chopped nuts on top.

Savor this oatmeal as a delightful way to start your day or as a comforting treat to enjoy during chilly mornings or cozy evenings.

Spiced Hot Chocolate Breakfast Smoothie with Banana and Almond Milk

Savor the rich and invigorating flavors of the Spiced Hot Chocolate Breakfast Smoothie, where the velvety smoothness of the banana and almond milk perfectly complements the warm and comforting notes of the Medieval Hot Chocolate Mix, creating a delightful and nourishing breakfast option that is both satisfying and energizing. Enjoy this smoothie as a wholesome and flavorful way to kick-start your day or as a delightful treat to enjoy during any time of the day.

Ingredients:

- 1 banana, frozen or fresh
- 2 tablespoons Medieval Hot Chocolate Mix
- 1 cup almond milk
- 1/4 teaspoon ground cinnamon
- 1/4 teaspoon ground nutmeg
- 1 tablespoon honey or maple syrup (optional, for added sweetness)
- Ice cubes (optional, if using a fresh banana)

Instructions:

1. In a blender, combine the banana, Medieval Hot Chocolate Mix, almond milk, ground cinnamon, and ground nutmeg.
2. If desired, add honey or maple syrup for additional sweetness.
3. Blend the ingredients on high speed until the mixture is smooth and creamy.
4. If you prefer a colder smoothie, you can add a handful of ice cubes to the blender and continue blending until the desired consistency is reached.
5. Pour the Spiced Hot Chocolate Breakfast Smoothie into a glass and sprinkle a pinch of ground cinnamon on top for garnish.

Warm Medieval Hot Chocolate Cinnamon Rolls with Cream Cheese Glaze

Imagine treating yourself to the delightful aroma of freshly baked Warm Medieval Hot Chocolate Cinnamon Rolls with Cream Cheese Glaze. As you take your first bite, the soft and pillowy texture of the cinnamon-infused dough envelops your senses, leaving behind a rich and indulgent taste that harkens back to the flavors of the medieval era.

The dough, crafted with care and precision, boasts the perfect balance of warmth from the hot chocolate mix, enhanced by a touch of cinnamon, nutmeg, and cloves. Each layer is generously spread with a luscious combination of softened butter, brown sugar, and a medley of aromatic spices, creating a swirl of tantalizing flavors in every bite.

As the rolls bake in the oven, the kitchen fills with the comforting scent of cinnamon and chocolate, promising a delightful treat that is both nostalgic and satisfying. The anticipation builds as the rolls rise and develop a golden, caramelized crust, revealing their tender and melt-in-your-mouth interior.

Once removed from the oven, the rolls are generously drizzled with a velvety cream cheese glaze, adding a creamy and tangy sweetness that beautifully balances the warm spices and the rich chocolate undertones. The smooth, decadent glaze complements the aromatic flavors, creating a harmonious blend that is sure to tantalize your taste buds and leave you longing for more.

Indulge in these Warm Medieval Hot Chocolate Cinnamon Rolls with Cream Cheese Glaze as a luxurious breakfast treat, a delectable dessert, or a delightful snack to be savored alongside a steaming cup of your favorite hot beverage. Transport yourself to a world of medieval charm and modern comfort with each delightful bite of these heavenly cinnamon rolls.

Ingredients:

For the Cinnamon Rolls:

- 1 package (1/4 ounce) active dry yeast
- 1 cup warm milk
- 1/2 cup granulated sugar
- 1/3 cup unsalted butter, melted
- 4 cups all-purpose flour
- 1/2 teaspoon salt
- 2 tablespoons Medieval Hot Chocolate Mix
- 1 large egg

For the Filling:

- 1/2 cup unsalted butter, softened
- 1 cup brown sugar
- 2 tablespoons ground cinnamon
- 1/2 teaspoon ground nutmeg
- 1/4 teaspoon ground cloves

For the Cream Cheese Glaze:

- 4 ounces cream cheese, softened
- 1/4 cup unsalted butter, softened
- 1 cup confectioners' sugar
- 1 teaspoon vanilla extract

Instructions:

1. In a large mixing bowl, dissolve the yeast in the warm milk and let it sit for about 5 minutes until frothy.
2. Add the sugar, melted butter, flour, salt, hot chocolate mix, and egg to the yeast mixture. Mix until the dough comes together.

3. Knead the dough on a floured surface for about 5 minutes until it becomes smooth and elastic.

4. Place the dough in a greased bowl, cover it, and let it rise in a warm place for about 1 hour, or until it doubles in size.

5. Roll out the dough on a floured surface into a large rectangle.

6. Spread the softened butter over the dough, then sprinkle the brown sugar, cinnamon, nutmeg, and cloves evenly over the butter.

7. Roll up the dough tightly from the long edge, then slice it into 12 equal-sized rolls.

8. Place the rolls in a greased baking dish and let them rise for an additional 30 minutes.

9. Preheat the oven to 375°F (190°C). Bake the rolls for 25-30 minutes, or until they are golden brown and cooked through.

10. While the rolls are baking, prepare the cream cheese glaze by beating the softened cream cheese, butter, confectioners' sugar, and vanilla extract until smooth and creamy.

11. Once the rolls are done, remove them from the oven and let them cool slightly. Drizzle the cream cheese glaze over the warm cinnamon rolls.

Enjoy these Warm Medieval Hot Chocolate Cinnamon Rolls with Cream Cheese Glaze as a delightful and indulgent treat, perfect for breakfast or as a comforting dessert option.

About Cinnamon in the Middle Ages

During the medieval period, cinnamon was a luxury item that was highly expensive and was often used by the upper classes to showcase their wealth and status. It was also commonly used in the preparation of elaborate feasts and banquets hosted by royalty and nobility, where its exotic and alluring aroma added a touch of sophistication to the culinary creations of the time.

Warm Medieval Hot Chocolate Crepes with Fresh Berries and Powdered Sugar

The origin of crepes can be traced back to the northwest region of France, particularly to the ancient region of Brittany. While the exact date of their creation remains uncertain, historical records suggest that crepes have been enjoyed in various forms for centuries.

Originally, crepes were called "galettes" and were made from buckwheat flour, which was abundant in the region. The process of making crepes was a simple and practical one, as they could be cooked quickly on large cast-iron hotplates. These thin, delicate pancakes were a staple of the Breton diet, often served with a variety of fillings, including meats, cheeses, and vegetables.

Over time, the popularity of crepes spread throughout France and eventually across Europe, where they were adapted to local culinary traditions and tastes. As they gained popularity, crepes became known for their versatility, as they could be enjoyed with both sweet and savory fillings, making them a popular dish for any meal of the day.

Today, crepes are celebrated worldwide for their delicate texture, diverse fillings, and the endless creative possibilities they offer. Whether enjoyed as a street food snack, a comforting breakfast, or an elegant dessert, crepes continue to be a beloved culinary delight that reflects the rich history and culinary heritage of France and beyond.

These Warm Medieval Hot Chocolate Crepes with Fresh Berries and Powdered Sugar offer a delightful combination of rich chocolate flavor, warm spices, and the natural sweetness of fresh berries. Enjoy these delectable crepes as a delightful and elegant dessert, perfect for a cozy evening or a special occasion.

Ingredients for the Crepes:

- 1 cup all-purpose flour
- 2 tablespoons Medieval Hot Chocolate Mix
- 2 large eggs
- 1 and 1/4 cups milk
- 2 tablespoons melted butter
- 1/4 teaspoon vanilla extract

For the Filling and Topping:

- Fresh berries of your choice (such as strawberries, raspberries, or blueberries)
- Powdered sugar for dusting
- Whipped cream or Greek yogurt (optional)

Instructions:

1. In a large mixing bowl, whisk together the all-purpose flour and Medieval Hot Chocolate Mix.
2. In a separate bowl, beat the eggs and milk together, then gradually add this mixture to the dry ingredients, whisking until smooth.
3. Stir in the melted butter and vanilla extract, ensuring the batter is well combined.
4. Heat a non-stick skillet or crepe pan over medium heat and lightly grease it with butter or oil.
5. Pour a small ladleful of batter into the skillet, swirling it around to create a thin, even layer. Cook for 1-2 minutes, or until the edges start to lift and the bottom is lightly golden. Flip and cook for an additional 1-2 minutes.
6. Remove the crepe from the pan and keep it warm. Repeat with the remaining batter.
7. Fill each crepe with a handful of fresh berries, fold or roll it up, and place it on a serving plate.
8. Dust the crepes with powdered sugar and top with a dollop of whipped cream or Greek yogurt if desired.

Cinnamon and Nutmeg Spiced Hot Chocolate Crème Brûlée

Savor the luscious and aromatic flavors of the Cinnamon and Nutmeg Spiced Hot Chocolate Crème Brûlée, where the rich and velvety custard harmonizes with the warm and comforting notes of the Medieval Hot Chocolate Mix, creating a dessert that is both indulgent and satisfying, perfect for adding a touch of elegance to any special occasion or for savoring as a luxurious treat to end a memorable meal.

Ingredients:

- 2 cups heavy cream
- 1/2 cup Medieval Hot Chocolate Mix
- 1 teaspoon ground cinnamon
- 1/2 teaspoon ground nutmeg
- 6 large egg yolks
- 1/4 cup granulated sugar, plus extra for caramelizing

Instructions:

1. Preheat your oven to 325°F (160°C). Place six ramekins in a large baking dish.
2. In a saucepan, heat the heavy cream, Medieval Hot Chocolate Mix, ground cinnamon, and ground nutmeg over medium heat, stirring constantly until the mixture is hot but not boiling. Remove from heat.
3. In a separate bowl, whisk the egg yolks and 1/4 cup granulated sugar until the mixture is thick and pale.
4. Slowly pour the hot cream mixture into the egg mixture, whisking constantly to prevent the eggs from scrambling.
5. Strain the mixture through a fine-mesh sieve into a large jug or bowl, then pour it evenly into the ramekins.
6. Place the baking dish in the oven and carefully pour hot water into the dish to come halfway up the sides of the ramekins.

7. Bake for 30-35 minutes, or until the edges are set but the centers are still slightly wobbly.

8. Remove the ramekins from the water bath and let them cool to room temperature. Then, refrigerate for at least 2 hours, or until they are thoroughly chilled.

9. Just before serving, sprinkle each chilled crème brûlée with a thin, even layer of granulated sugar. Use a kitchen torch to caramelize the sugar until it forms a crisp and golden-brown crust.

§

Cinnamon and Nutmeg Spiced Hot Chocolate Scones with Clotted Cream

These Cinnamon and Nutmeg Spiced Hot Chocolate Scones with Clotted Cream offer a delightful twist on the classic scone, infusing it with the rich flavors of hot chocolate and warm spices. Enjoy these tender and flavorful scones as a delightful addition to your breakfast or afternoon tea, perfectly complemented by the luxurious richness of clotted cream.

Ingredients:

- 2 cups all-purpose flour
- 1 tablespoon baking powder
- 1/2 teaspoon ground nutmeg
- 1/2 cup Medieval Hot Chocolate Mix
- 1/2 cup unsalted butter, cold and cut into small pieces
- 1/2 cup buttermilk
- 1 large egg
- 1 teaspoon vanilla extract
- Clotted cream, for serving

Instructions:

1. Preheat your oven to 400°F (200°C). Line a baking sheet with parchment paper.

2. In a large mixing bowl, whisk together the flour, sugar, baking powder, salt, cinnamon, nutmeg, and cocoa powder until well combined.

3. Add the cold butter pieces to the dry ingredients and use a pastry cutter or your fingertips to cut the butter into the flour mixture until it resembles coarse crumbs.

4. In a separate bowl, whisk together the buttermilk, egg, and vanilla extract.

5. Gradually pour the wet ingredients into the dry ingredients and mix until just combined.

6. Turn the dough out onto a floured surface and gently knead it a few times until it comes together.

7. Pat the dough into a circle that's about 1-inch thick. Use a sharp knife to cut the circle into 8 wedges.

8. Place the scones on the prepared baking sheet and bake for 15-18 minutes, or until they are lightly golden.

9. Remove the scones from the oven and let them cool slightly on a wire rack.

10. Serve the Cinnamon and Nutmeg Spiced Hot Chocolate Scones with Clotted Cream, and enjoy the delightful combination of warm, spiced flavors and the rich, creamy texture of clotted cream.

§

Cinnamon and Sugar Dusted Medieval Hot Chocolate Donuts

The term "doughnut" can be traced back to the early 19th century in America, but the concept of fried dough has much deeper historical roots, with the Middle Ages serving as a crucial era for the development and popularization of various fried dough treats that eventually contributed to the evolution of the modern-day donut.

These Cinnamon and Sugar Dusted Medieval Hot Chocolate Donuts offer a delightful twist on the classic treat, infusing them with the rich flavors of hot chocolate and warm medieval spices. Enjoy these delectable donuts as a delightful breakfast or as a comforting snack, perfect for enjoying with a warm beverage or on their own.

Ingredients:

For the Donuts:

- 2 cups all-purpose flour
- 1/2 cup granulated sugar
- 1/4 cup Medieval Hot Chocolate Mix
- 2 teaspoons baking powder
- 1/2 teaspoon baking soda
- 1/2 teaspoon salt
- 3/4 cup buttermilk
- 2 large eggs
- 2 tablespoons unsalted butter, melted
- 1 teaspoon vanilla extract

For the Topping:

- 1/2 cup granulated sugar
- 1 tablespoon ground cinnamon
- 4 tablespoons unsalted butter, melted

Instructions:

1. Preheat your oven to 350°F (175°C). Grease a donut pan and set it aside.
2. In a large mixing bowl, whisk together the flour, sugar, cocoa powder, baking powder, baking soda, cinnamon, nutmeg, cloves, and salt.
3. In a separate bowl, whisk together the buttermilk, eggs, melted butter, and vanilla extract.
4. Gradually add the wet ingredients to the dry ingredients, stirring until just combined.
5. Spoon the batter into a piping bag or a large resealable plastic bag with a corner snipped off.

6. Pipe the batter into the prepared donut pan, filling each cavity about 2/3 full.
7. Bake for 10-12 minutes, or until the donuts spring back when lightly pressed.
8. While the donuts are baking, prepare the topping by combining the granulated sugar and ground cinnamon in a shallow bowl.
9. Remove the donuts from the oven and let them cool for a few minutes. Dip each donut in the melted butter, then roll it in the cinnamon-sugar mixture until fully coated.
10. Serve the Cinnamon and Sugar Dusted Medieval Hot Chocolate Donuts and enjoy their rich, spiced flavor and delightful sugary coating.

§

Cinnamon and Nutmeg Spiced Medieval Hot Chocolate Cheesecake

Enjoy this decadent Cinnamon and Nutmeg Spiced Medieval Hot Chocolate Cheesecake as a luxurious and indulgent dessert, perfect for special occasions or as a delightful treat to share with friends and family.

Ingredients:

For the Crust:

- 1 and 1/2 cups graham cracker crumbs
- 1/4 1/4 cup Medieval Hot Chocolate Mix
- 1/2 cup unsalted butter, melted

For the Cheesecake Filling:

- 24 ounces cream cheese, softened
- 1 cup granulated sugar
- 3 large eggs
- 1 cup sour cream

- 1/4 cup 1/4 cup Medieval Hot Chocolate Mix
- 1 teaspoon vanilla extract
For the Topping:

- Whipped cream
- Ground cinnamon and nutmeg, for garnish

Instructions:

1. Preheat your oven to 325°F (165°C). Grease a 9-inch springform pan and set it aside.
2. In a medium bowl, combine the graham cracker crumbs, sugar, cinnamon, and nutmeg. Stir in the melted butter until the mixture resembles wet sand.
3. Press the crumb mixture firmly and evenly into the bottom of the prepared springform pan.
4. In a large mixing bowl, beat the cream cheese and sugar together until smooth and creamy.
5. Add the eggs one at a time, mixing well after each addition.
6. Stir in the sour cream, cocoa powder, vanilla extract, cinnamon, nutmeg, and cloves until the batter is smooth and well combined.
7. Pour the cheesecake filling over the crust in the springform pan.
8. Bake for 45-50 minutes, or until the center is set and the edges are slightly golden.
9. Turn off the oven and let the cheesecake cool inside for 1 hour, then transfer it to a wire rack to cool completely.
10. Once cooled, refrigerate the cheesecake for at least 4 hours or overnight.
11. Before serving, garnish the Cinnamon and Nutmeg Spiced Medieval Hot Chocolate Cheesecake with whipped cream and a sprinkle of ground cinnamon and nutmeg.

Medieval Hot Chocolate Flavored Bread and Butter Pudding with Raisins

This Medieval Hot Chocolate Flavored Bread and Butter Pudding with Raisins offers a delightful blend of warm and comforting flavors, combining the rich essence of hot chocolate with the sweetness of raisins, creating a satisfying and indulgent dessert that is perfect for sharing with loved ones.

Ingredients:

- 6 cups day-old bread, cut into cubes
- 1/2 cup raisins
- 4 tablespoons unsalted butter, softened
- 4 large eggs
- 2 cups whole milk
- 1/2 cup heavy cream
- 1/2 1/4 cup Medieval Hot Chocolate Mix
- 1 teaspoon vanilla extract
- Pinch of salt

Instructions:

1. Preheat your oven to 350°F (175°C). Grease a baking dish and set it aside.
2. Place the bread cubes and raisins in the prepared baking dish.
3. Spread the softened butter over each bread cube.
4. In a large mixing bowl, whisk together the eggs, milk, heavy cream, sugar, vanilla extract, cocoa powder, cinnamon, nutmeg, and a pinch of salt.
5. Pour the egg mixture over the bread cubes, ensuring that all the bread is soaked in the liquid.
6. Let the bread mixture sit for about 15-20 minutes, allowing the bread to absorb the custard.
7. Bake the bread and butter pudding for 35-40 minutes, or until the top is golden and the custard is set.

8. Remove the pudding from the oven and let it cool slightly before serving.
9. Serve the Medieval Hot Chocolate Flavored Bread and Butter Pudding with Raisins warm, and enjoy the comforting and rich flavors reminiscent of the medieval era.

§

Medieval Hot Chocolate Flavored Churros with Cinnamon Sugar

Churros, as we know them today, did not specifically exist in the Middle Ages. The origins of churros are often attributed to Spanish shepherds, who created a simple fried dough pastry that was easy to make and cook over an open fire during their long journeys in the mountains.

However, during the Middle Ages in Spain, there were similar fried dough pastries and treats that served as predecessors to the churros we know today. These treats were often made by frying dough in oil and were commonly sweetened with honey, sugar, or a combination of both. While not identical to modern churros, these early versions laid the foundation for the development of the popular Spanish churro.

Over time, churros evolved into the elongated, ridged shape that is now synonymous with this beloved Spanish dessert. Churros are typically made from a simple dough, piped through a star-shaped nozzle to achieve their signature ridged texture, deep-fried until crispy and golden, and traditionally dusted with sugar or cinnamon. They are often served with a rich and thick hot chocolate dip, which has become a classic accompaniment for enjoying churros in Spain and around the world.

Despite their more recent origins, churros have become an iconic part of Spanish culinary culture, enjoyed as a delicious snack, dessert, or breakfast item in Spain and many other countries worldwide.

Ingredients:

For the Churros:

- 1 cup water
- 1/2 cup unsalted butter
- 2 tablespoons granulated sugar
- 1/4 teaspoon salt
- 1 cup all-purpose flour
- 2 large eggs
- 1 teaspoon vanilla extract
- 1/4 cup 1/4 cup Medieval Hot Chocolate Mix
- Vegetable oil, for frying

For the Cinnamon Sugar Coating:

- 1/2 cup granulated sugar
- 1 tablespoon ground cinnamon

Instructions:

1. In a saucepan, combine the water, butter, sugar, and salt. Bring the mixture to a boil over medium heat.
2. Reduce the heat to low, and add the flour all at once. Stir vigorously until the mixture forms a ball and pulls away from the sides of the pan.
3. Transfer the dough to a mixing bowl and let it cool for a few minutes.
4. Beat the eggs into the dough one at a time, ensuring that each egg is fully incorporated before adding the next.
5. Stir in the vanilla extract and cocoa powder until the dough is smooth and uniform.

6. Heat the vegetable oil in a large, heavy-bottomed pot to 375°F (190°C).

7. Spoon the dough into a piping bag fitted with a large star tip.

8. Pipe 4-6 inch strips of dough directly into the hot oil, using a knife or scissors to cut the dough from the piping tip.

9. Fry the churros for 2-3 minutes, or until they are golden brown and crispy.

10. Remove the churros from the oil and let them drain on a paper towel-lined plate.

11. In a shallow bowl, mix together the granulated sugar and ground cinnamon for the coating.

12. Roll the warm churros in the cinnamon sugar mixture until they are evenly coated.

13. Serve the Medieval Hot Chocolate Flavored Churros with Cinnamon Sugar immediately, and enjoy their rich, chocolatey flavor combined with the warm spice of cinnamon.

§

Medieval Hot Chocolate Flavored Chocolate Chip Cookies with Sea Salt

Sea salt has been used as an essential ingredient throughout history, including during the Middle Ages. It was a highly prized and valuable commodity in many regions, used not only for culinary purposes but also for various other applications, including food preservation and medicinal practices.

During the Middle Ages, sea salt was a crucial element in preserving food, especially meats and fish, before the advent of refrigeration. It was commonly used to cure and preserve food items, allowing them to be stored for extended periods without spoiling. This was particularly important during the winter months and for long journeys, ensuring a steady supply of nourishment even in times of scarcity.

Furthermore, sea salt was used to enhance the flavor of dishes, as it was known for its ability to bring out the natural flavors of foods and ingredients. Its distinct taste and texture made it an important seasoning in both savory and sweet dishes, adding depth and complexity to various culinary creations.

Sea salt was also used in various medicinal practices during the Middle Ages. It was believed to possess cleansing and purifying properties, making it a common ingredient in medicinal remedies and treatments for a wide range of ailments.

Overall, sea salt played a vital role in the culinary and medicinal practices of the Middle Ages, and its significance as a valuable ingredient and commodity has persisted throughout history, making it a staple in kitchens and households around the world even to this day.

Enjoy these Medieval Hot Chocolate Flavored Chocolate Chip Cookies with Sea Salt as a delightful treat, combining the rich flavors of hot chocolate with the comforting familiarity of classic chocolate chip cookies, elevated with a touch of sea salt for a perfect balance of sweet and salty flavors.

Ingredients:

- 1 cup (2 sticks) unsalted butter, softened
- 1 cup granulated sugar
- 1 cup packed brown sugar
- 2 large eggs

- 1 teaspoon vanilla extract
- 2 cups all-purpose flour
- 1/2 cup unsweetened cocoa powder
- 1 teaspoon baking soda
- 1/2 teaspoon salt
- 1/8 cup Medieval Hot Chocolate Mix
- 1 and 1/2 cups semisweet chocolate chips
- Sea salt, for sprinkling

Instructions:

1. Preheat your oven to 375°F (190°C). Line baking sheets with parchment paper and set aside.
2. In a large mixing bowl, cream together the softened butter, granulated sugar, and brown sugar until light and fluffy.
3. Beat in the eggs one at a time, then stir in the vanilla extract.
4. In a separate bowl, whisk together the flour, cocoa powder, baking soda, salt, cinnamon, nutmeg, and cloves.
5. Gradually add the dry ingredients to the wet ingredients, mixing until just combined.
6. Fold in the semisweet chocolate chips until they are evenly distributed throughout the dough.
7. Drop rounded tablespoons of dough onto the prepared baking sheets.
8. Sprinkle a small pinch of sea salt on top of each cookie dough mound.
9. Bake the cookies for 8-10 minutes, or until they are set around the edges but still slightly soft in the center.
10. Remove the cookies from the oven and let them cool on the baking sheets for a few minutes before transferring them to a wire rack to cool completely.

Medieval Hot Chocolate Flavored Panna Cotta with Dark Chocolate Shavings

Visualize the enchanting allure of a dessert that embodies the essence of the medieval era, the Medieval Hot Chocolate Flavored Panna Cotta with Dark Chocolate Shavings. As you gaze upon the delicate, velvety texture and rich, deep hue of the Panna Cotta, you are drawn into a world of decadent indulgence and sophisticated flavors.

With each spoonful, your palate is enveloped in the luxurious creaminess of the Panna Cotta, where the intricate blend of heavy cream, whole milk, and fragrant vanilla extract creates a luscious base for the infusion of the exquisite hot chocolate essence. The interplay of unsweetened cocoa powder, warming cinnamon, tantalizing nutmeg, and subtle hints of cloves dance harmoniously on your taste buds, delivering a symphony of rich, aromatic flavors that evoke the opulence and grandeur of the medieval courts.

The sensation of the smooth, silken texture is heightened by the delicate firmness, offering a luxurious mouthfeel that delicately melts on your tongue, leaving behind a trail of indulgent satisfaction. The final touch of decadence comes in the form of dark chocolate shavings, lending a delicate bitterness that perfectly complements the creamy sweetness of the Panna Cotta, elevating each spoonful into a realm of unparalleled delight.

Indulge in the enchanting Medieval Hot Chocolate Flavored Panna Cotta with Dark Chocolate Shavings, a dessert that transcends time, offering a moment of pure bliss and sensory delight, perfect for relishing during intimate gatherings or as a sophisticated finale to a memorable dining experience.

Ingredients:

- 2 cups heavy cream
- 1 cup whole milk
- 1/2 cup granulated sugar
- 1 teaspoon vanilla extract
- 1/4 1/4 cup Medieval Hot Chocolate Mix
- 2 packets (about 4 1/2 teaspoons) powdered gelatin
- 2 tablespoons cold water
- Dark chocolate shavings, for garnish

Instructions:

1. In a saucepan, combine the heavy cream, whole milk, sugar, and vanilla extract. Heat the mixture over medium heat, stirring occasionally, until it is hot but not boiling.
2. In a separate bowl, whisk together the cocoa powder, cinnamon, nutmeg, and cloves.
3. Gradually whisk the cocoa mixture into the hot cream mixture until it is fully incorporated. Remove from heat and set aside.
4. In a small bowl, sprinkle the powdered gelatin over the cold water and let it sit for about 5 minutes to soften.
5. Once the gelatin has softened, gently heat it in the microwave for a few seconds or on the stovetop until it is fully dissolved.
6. Stir the dissolved gelatin into the hot cream mixture until it is well combined.
7. Pour the Panna Cotta mixture into individual serving glasses or ramekins.
8. Refrigerate the Panna Cotta for at least 4 hours, or until it is set and firm.
9. Before serving, garnish each Panna Cotta with a generous amount of dark chocolate shavings.

Medieval Hot Chocolate Flavored Tiramisu with Cocoa and Mascarpone

Indulge in the sumptuous delight of this Medieval Hot Chocolate Flavored Tiramisu with Cocoa and Mascarpone, a decadent dessert that marries the rich, warming flavors of hot chocolate with the timeless elegance of traditional Tiramisu. Savor each spoonful of this luscious creation, celebrating the harmonious blend of creamy mascarpone, delicate ladyfingers, and the indulgent essence of cocoa and aromatic spices, transporting you to a realm of culinary bliss and timeless indulgence.

Ingredients:

- 1 cup strong brewed coffee, cooled
- 2 tablespoons rum or coffee liqueur (optional)
- 24 ladyfinger cookies
- 3 large eggs, separated
- 3/4 cup granulated sugar, divided
- 1 teaspoon vanilla extract
- 8 ounces mascarpone cheese
- 1 cup heavy cream
- 1/4 1/4 cup Medieval Hot Chocolate Mix

Instructions:

1. In a shallow dish, combine the cooled coffee and rum or coffee liqueur, if using.
2. Quickly dip each ladyfinger into the coffee mixture, making sure not to soak them, and line the bottom of an 8x8 inch dish with a layer of the dipped ladyfingers.
3. In a large mixing bowl, beat the egg yolks with 1/2 cup of sugar until the mixture is thick and pale. Stir in the vanilla extract.
4. In a separate bowl, whisk the mascarpone cheese until it is smooth and creamy.

5. In another bowl, whip the heavy cream until it forms stiff peaks.
6. Gently fold the whipped cream into the mascarpone cheese.
7. In a separate bowl, beat the egg whites with the remaining 1/4 cup of sugar until they form stiff peaks.
8. Gently fold the beaten egg whites into the mascarpone mixture until fully combined.
9. In a small bowl, combine the cocoa powder, cinnamon, nutmeg, and cloves.
10. Sprinkle a layer of the cocoa and spice mixture over the layer of dipped ladyfingers.
11. Spread half of the mascarpone mixture over the cocoa and spice layer.
12. Repeat the layers with the remaining ladyfingers, coffee mixture, cocoa and spice mixture, and mascarpone mixture.
13. Cover the dish and refrigerate the Tiramisu for at least 4 hours, or overnight, to allow the flavors to meld.

§

Medieval Hot Chocolate Flavored Yogurt Parfait with Granola and Honey

Enjoy this delightful Medieval Hot Chocolate Flavored Yogurt Parfait with Granola and Honey as a wholesome and satisfying breakfast or as a delightful snack to savor during a tranquil moment. Revel in the luxurious blend of creamy yogurt infused with the comforting flavors of hot chocolate, enhanced by the delicate sweetness of honey and the delightful crunch of granola, creating a parfait that is both nourishing and indulgent.

Ingredients:

- 2 cups plain Greek yogurt
- 2 tablespoons honey
- 1/4 cup Medieval Hot Chocolate Mix

- 1 cup granola
- 1/2 cup mixed berries (such as strawberries, blueberries, or raspberries)
- Additional honey, for drizzling

Instructions:

1. In a mixing bowl, combine the plain Greek yogurt, unsweetened cocoa powder, honey, cinnamon, nutmeg, and cloves. Stir until the cocoa powder is fully incorporated and the mixture is smooth.
2. In serving glasses or jars, layer the yogurt mixture with the granola and mixed berries, creating alternating layers of creamy yogurt, crunchy granola, and juicy berries.
3. Repeat the layering process until the glasses or jars are filled, finishing with a layer of yogurt on top.
4. Drizzle a small amount of honey over the top layer of yogurt.
5. Optionally, garnish with additional berries and a sprinkle of granola for added texture and visual appeal.

§

Medieval Hot Chocolate Infused Chocolate Bark with Almonds and Sea Salt

Indulge in the rich and nuanced flavors of this Medieval Hot Chocolate Infused Chocolate Bark with Almonds and Sea Salt, offering a delightful blend of decadent dark chocolate infused with the nostalgic essence of the pre-made hot chocolate mix, heightened by the delightful crunch of toasted almonds and the delicate savory touch of sea salt. Enjoy this exquisite treat as a luxurious indulgence to savor during a peaceful moment or as an elegant gift to share with friends and loved ones.

Ingredients:

- 10 ounces dark chocolate, chopped
- 1/4 cup Medieval Hot Chocolate Mix
- 1 cup whole almonds, toasted and roughly chopped
- Sea salt, for sprinkling

Instructions:

1. Line a baking sheet with parchment paper and set it aside.
2. In a heatproof bowl set over a pot of simmering water, melt the dark chocolate, stirring occasionally, until it is smooth and completely melted.
3. Remove the melted chocolate from the heat and stir in the pre-made hot chocolate mix until it is fully incorporated.
4. Quickly stir in the toasted and chopped almonds until they are well coated with the chocolate mixture.
5. Pour the chocolate and almond mixture onto the prepared baking sheet and spread it out into an even layer with a spatula.
6. Sprinkle a small amount of sea salt evenly over the surface of the chocolate bark.
7. Place the baking sheet in the refrigerator for about 30 minutes, or until the chocolate is set.
8. Once set, break the chocolate bark into pieces of your desired size and shape.

§

Medieval Hot Chocolate Infused Chocolate Truffles with Cocoa Powder

Enjoy these exquisite Medieval Hot Chocolate Infused Chocolate Truffles with Cocoa Powder, where the richness of the dark chocolate is beautifully complemented by the nostalgic flavors of the Medieval Hot Chocolate Mix. Savor these delectable truffles as a luxurious indulgence to enjoy during a peaceful moment or as an elegant treat to share with friends and loved ones.

Ingredients:

- 8 ounces dark chocolate, finely chopped
- 1/2 cup heavy cream
- 2 tablespoons butter, softened
- 2 tablespoons Medieval Hot Chocolate Mix
- Cocoa powder, for rolling

Instructions:

1. Place the finely chopped dark chocolate in a heatproof bowl.
2. In a saucepan, heat the heavy cream over medium heat until it begins to simmer.
3. Pour the hot cream over the chopped chocolate and let it sit for 1-2 minutes.
4. Stir the chocolate and cream mixture until the chocolate is completely melted and the mixture is smooth and glossy.
5. Add the softened butter and Medieval Hot Chocolate Mix to the chocolate mixture. Stir until all the ingredients are well combined and the mixture is homogeneous.
6. Cover the bowl with plastic wrap and refrigerate for 2-3 hours, or until the mixture is firm enough to handle.
7. Using a spoon or a small cookie scoop, scoop out portions of the chilled chocolate mixture and roll them into small balls.
8. Roll the truffles in cocoa powder until they are evenly coated.
9. Place the coated truffles on a parchment-lined baking sheet and refrigerate for another 30 minutes to set.

Medieval Hot Chocolate Infused Pecan Pie with Whipped Cream

Enjoy the rich and decadent flavors of this Medieval Hot Chocolate Infused Pecan Pie, where the warm and aromatic essence of the hot chocolate mix beautifully complements the sweet and nutty flavors of the classic pecan pie, creating a delightful dessert that is perfect for special occasions or a comforting treat during the cooler seasons.

Ingredients:

For the Pie Crust:

- 1 and 1/4 cups all-purpose flour
- 1/2 teaspoon salt
- 1/2 cup unsalted butter, cold and cubed
- 3-4 tablespoons ice water

For the Filling:

- 1 cup Medieval Hot Chocolate Mix
- 1 cup corn syrup
- 3 eggs
- 1 teaspoon vanilla extract
- 1 cup pecan halves

For the Whipped Cream:

- 1 cup heavy cream
- 2 tablespoons powdered sugar
- 1 teaspoon vanilla extract

Instructions:

1. For the Pie Crust: In a food processor, pulse the flour and salt. Add the cold, cubed butter and pulse until

the mixture resembles coarse crumbs. Gradually add the ice water, one tablespoon at a time, and pulse until the dough comes together. Shape the dough into a disc, wrap it in plastic wrap, and refrigerate for at least 30 minutes.

2. Preheat the oven to 350°F (175°C).

3. On a floured surface, roll out the chilled dough into a circle and carefully transfer it to a 9-inch pie dish. Trim and crimp the edges as desired.

4. For the Filling: In a large bowl, whisk together the Medieval Hot Chocolate Mix, corn syrup, eggs, and vanilla extract until well combined. Stir in the pecan halves.

5. Pour the filling into the prepared pie crust.

6. Bake the pie for 50-60 minutes, or until the filling is set and the crust is golden brown. If the crust starts to brown too quickly, cover the edges with foil.

7. For the Whipped Cream: In a large bowl, beat the heavy cream, powdered sugar, and vanilla extract until soft peaks form.

8. Serve the Medieval Hot Chocolate Infused Pecan Pie with dollops of whipped cream on top.

§

Medieval Hot Chocolate Infused Waffles with Fresh Berries and Cream

Enjoy these delightful Medieval Hot Chocolate Infused Waffles with Fresh Berries and Cream, where the nostalgic flavors of the hot chocolate mix perfectly complement the fluffy and indulgent waffles, creating a delightful breakfast or brunch option that is perfect for enjoying with friends and family, or as a special treat to brighten up your mornings.

Ingredients:

For the Waffles:

- 1 and 1/2 cups all-purpose flour
- 3 tablespoons Medieval Hot Chocolate Mix
- 2 teaspoons baking powder
- 1/2 teaspoon baking soda
- 1/4 teaspoon salt
- 2 large eggs
- 1 and 1/4 cups buttermilk
- 1/4 cup unsalted butter, melted
- 1 teaspoon vanilla extract

For the Topping:

- Fresh mixed berries (such as strawberries, blueberries, raspberries, or blackberries)
- Whipped cream
- Maple syrup or honey, for drizzling

Instructions:

1. Preheat your waffle iron according to the manufacturer's instructions.
2. In a large mixing bowl, whisk together the flour, Medieval Hot Chocolate Mix, baking powder, baking soda, and salt.
3. In another bowl, whisk the eggs, buttermilk, melted butter, and vanilla extract until well combined.
4. Pour the wet ingredients into the bowl with the dry ingredients and stir until just combined. The batter should be slightly lumpy.
5. Cook the waffles according to the waffle iron instructions until they are golden and crisp.
6. Top the waffles with a generous amount of fresh mixed berries and a dollop of whipped cream.
7. Drizzle the waffles with maple syrup or honey to taste.

Spiced Hot Chocolate Chia Seed Pudding with Coconut Flakes

Imagine delighting in a captivating bowl of Spiced Hot Chocolate Chia Seed Pudding with Coconut Flakes, a culinary masterpiece that seamlessly blends the comfort of a classic hot chocolate with the wholesome goodness of chia seeds and the nutty allure of toasted coconut. As you take your first spoonful, the luscious creaminess of the pudding envelops your senses, carrying the warm and aromatic notes of cinnamon, nutmeg, and cloves that dance harmoniously with the rich, indulgent essence of cocoa.

Each spoonful presents a satisfying texture, a delightful interplay of the velvety smoothness of the pudding and the gentle crunch of the chia seeds, offering a symphony of sensations that culminate in a truly gratifying experience. The toasted coconut flakes, golden and fragrant, add a subtle yet distinctive nuttiness that elevates the flavor profile, providing a delightful contrast to the rich chocolatey base.

This Spiced Hot Chocolate Chia Seed Pudding with Coconut Flakes serves not only as a delightful indulgence but also as a wholesome and nourishing option, perfect for starting your day with a touch of decadence or for winding down with a guilt-free dessert. Allow yourself to be embraced by the comforting warmth of the spiced hot chocolate, the wholesome texture of the chia seeds, and the delightful nuttiness of the toasted coconut, creating a moment of pure bliss and sensory delight with every spoonful.

Ingredients:

- 1/4 cup chia seeds
- 1 and 1/2 cups milk (or a non-dairy alternative of your choice)
- 2 tablespoons honey or maple syrup

- 5 tablespoons Medieval Hot Chocolate Mix
- 1/4 cup coconut flakes

Instructions:

1. In a bowl, combine the chia seeds, milk, honey or maple syrup, cocoa powder, cinnamon, nutmeg, cloves, and vanilla extract. Mix well to ensure the cocoa powder is fully incorporated and no lumps remain.
2. Cover the bowl and refrigerate the mixture for at least 4 hours, or preferably overnight, to allow the chia seeds to absorb the liquid and thicken into a pudding-like consistency.
3. Stir the mixture again before serving to ensure even distribution of the chia seeds.
4. Toast the coconut flakes in a dry skillet over medium heat until they are golden and fragrant.
5. Sprinkle the toasted coconut flakes over the top of the chilled spiced hot chocolate chia seed pudding.
6. Serve the pudding chilled and enjoy the delightful blend of comforting hot chocolate flavors combined with the satisfying texture of chia seeds and the nutty, aromatic essence of toasted coconut flakes.

Indulge in this exquisite Spiced Hot Chocolate Chia Seed Pudding with Coconut Flakes, a delightful and wholesome treat that can be enjoyed as a nourishing breakfast option, a satisfying snack, or a guilt-free dessert.

§

Spiced Hot Chocolate Mug Cake with Vanilla Ice Cream

Indulge in the rich and aromatic flavors of a Spiced Hot Chocolate Mug Cake, infused with the warm essence of the Medieval Hot Chocolate Mix. This delectable treat offers a delightful combination of aromatic spices, including cinnamon and nutmeg, creating a tantalizing aroma that fills the air as it bakes to perfection in a cozy mug.

As the mug cake rises, the kitchen is enveloped in the comforting scent of chocolate and spices, evoking feelings of warmth and contentment. The luscious, moist cake, with its delicate crumb and decadent texture, is a delightful contrast to the cool, velvety scoop of vanilla ice cream melting gently over the top.

With each spoonful, savor the harmonious blend of sweet and spiced flavors, as the rich chocolate notes mingle with the comforting warmth of cinnamon and nutmeg, creating a truly indulgent experience. The cool creaminess of the vanilla ice cream provides a luxurious and refreshing complement to the decadent mug cake, offering a delightful contrast that tantalizes the taste buds and leaves a lasting impression of sweet bliss.

Ingredients:

- 4 tablespoons all-purpose flour
- 2 tablespoons Medieval Hot Chocolate Mix
- 1/4 teaspoon baking powder
- 1/8 teaspoon baking soda
- Pinch of salt
- 3 tablespoons milk
- 2 tablespoons vegetable oil
- 1/4 teaspoon vanilla extract
- 1 tablespoon hot water
- 1 scoop vanilla ice cream

Instructions:

1. In a microwave-safe mug, whisk together the all-purpose flour, Medieval Hot Chocolate Mix, baking powder, baking soda, and salt until well combined.
2. Add the milk, vegetable oil, and vanilla extract to the dry ingredients and mix until the batter is smooth.

3. Stir in the hot water until fully incorporated.
4. Microwave the mug on high for 60-70 seconds, or until the cake is set but still moist.
5. Allow the mug cake to cool for a minute before adding a scoop of vanilla ice cream on top.
6. Serve the Spiced Hot Chocolate Mug Cake with a dollop of vanilla ice cream melting into the warm, spiced cake, creating a decadent and comforting treat that is perfect for satisfying your sweet tooth on cozy evenings or for enjoying a delightful dessert with a touch of indulgence.

§

Warm Medieval Hot Chocolate Bread Pudding with Vanilla Sauce

Picture indulging in a delightful serving of Warm Medieval Hot Chocolate Bread Pudding with Vanilla Sauce, a decadent treat that seamlessly marries the nostalgic essence of the medieval era with the comforting allure of a classic bread pudding. As you take your first bite, the luscious and velvety texture of the pudding envelops your palate, revealing a symphony of flavors that dance harmoniously together. The subtle warmth of cinnamon, nutmeg, and cloves, intricately woven into the Medieval Hot Chocolate Mix, gently mingles with the soft, custard-like bread cubes, creating a sensation that is both familiar and delightfully novel.

Each spoonful unveils a medley of textures and tastes, where the tender raisins or dried cranberries, if included, provide delightful bursts of sweetness that contrast beautifully with the rich, indulgent flavors of the bread pudding. As the vanilla sauce delicately cascades over the warm pudding, its sweet aroma wafts through the air, heralding the final touch of decadence that brings the entire dish together.

Fun fact: Bread pudding has been a popular dish for centuries, with its origins dating back to the early 11th and 12th centuries when frugal cooks sought ways to utilize leftover bread. This enduring dessert has evolved across cultures, and variations can be found in cuisines around the world, each with its unique twist and flavor profile, making it a beloved comfort food for many. Enjoy this Warm Medieval Hot Chocolate Bread Pudding with Vanilla Sauce as a delightful homage to the rich culinary history of this timeless dessert, perfect for creating heartwarming moments and cherished memories with your loved ones.

Ingredients for the Bread Pudding:

- 6 cups day-old bread, cut into cubes
- 2 cups milk
- 4 eggs
- 1/2 cup Medieval Hot Chocolate Mix
- 1/4 cup unsalted butter, melted
- 1 teaspoon vanilla extract
- 1/2 cup raisins or dried cranberries (optional)

Ingredients for the Vanilla Sauce:

- 1 cup heavy cream
- 2 tablespoons granulated sugar
- 1 teaspoon vanilla extract

Instructions:

1. Preheat your oven to 350°F (175°C) and grease a baking dish.
2. In a large bowl, combine the bread cubes and milk, allowing the bread to soak up the milk for about 10 minutes.
3. In a separate bowl, whisk together the eggs, Medieval Hot Chocolate Mix, melted butter, and vanilla extract until well combined.

4. Pour the egg mixture over the bread and milk mixture, and add the raisins or dried cranberries if desired. Stir gently to combine.

5. Transfer the bread pudding mixture to the greased baking dish and bake for 35-40 minutes, or until the top is golden and the pudding is set.

6. While the bread pudding is baking, prepare the vanilla sauce. In a small saucepan, heat the heavy cream and granulated sugar over medium heat, stirring constantly, until the sugar has dissolved. Remove from heat and stir in the vanilla extract.

7. Once the bread pudding is done, serve it warm with a drizzle of the vanilla sauce on top.

Enjoy the luscious and comforting flavors of this Warm Medieval Hot Chocolate Bread Pudding with Vanilla Sauce, where the rich and aromatic essence of the Medieval Hot Chocolate Mix beautifully complements the soft and indulgent texture of the bread pudding, creating a delightful dessert that is perfect for cozy evenings or as a delightful treat to share with friends and loved ones.

§

Warm Medieval Hot Chocolate Custard with Caramelized Sugar Topping

Savor the rich and velvety texture of this Warm Medieval Hot Chocolate Custard with its delightful caramelized sugar topping, where the intricate blend of the Medieval Hot Chocolate Mix infuses each spoonful with a comforting and indulgent warmth, creating a dessert that is perfect for rounding off a memorable meal or for enjoying as a luxurious treat on special occasions.

Ingredients for the Custard:

- 2 cups whole milk
- 1/2 cup heavy cream
- 1/2 cup Medieval Hot Chocolate Mix
- 4 large eggs
- 1 teaspoon vanilla extract

Ingredients for the Caramelized Sugar Topping:

- 1/4 cup granulated sugar
- 2 tablespoons water

Instructions:

1. Preheat your oven to 325°F (165°C) and prepare 4 ramekins by greasing them lightly.
2. In a saucepan, heat the milk and heavy cream over medium heat until it begins to simmer. Remove from heat and whisk in the Medieval Hot Chocolate Mix until fully dissolved.
3. In a separate bowl, whisk the eggs and vanilla extract together until well combined.
4. Gradually pour the hot chocolate mixture into the eggs, whisking constantly to prevent the eggs from cooking.
5. Divide the custard mixture evenly among the ramekins.
6. Place the ramekins in a large baking dish and fill the dish with enough hot water to reach halfway up the sides of the ramekins.
7. Carefully transfer the baking dish to the preheated oven and bake for 30-35 minutes, or until the custard is set around the edges but slightly jiggly in the center.
8. Remove the ramekins from the water bath and let them cool to room temperature. Then, refrigerate the custards for at least 2 hours, or until they are thoroughly chilled.
9. Just before serving, prepare the caramelized sugar topping. In a small saucepan, combine the granulated

sugar and water over medium-high heat, swirling the
pan occasionally until the sugar caramelizes and turns
golden brown.
10. Drizzle the caramelized sugar over the chilled
custards, allowing it to harden into a crisp topping.

§

Warm Medieval Hot Chocolate Pudding with Whipped Cream

Enjoy the delightful contrast between the warm,
decadent pudding and the light, airy whipped cream,
as the rich and comforting flavors of the Medieval Hot
Chocolate Mix infuse each spoonful with a delightful
essence that is perfect for satisfying your sweet tooth
on cozy evenings or for enjoying a delightful dessert
with a touch of indulgence.

Ingredients for the Pudding:

- 1 cup all-purpose flour
- 1/2 cup granulated sugar
- 2 tablespoons Medieval Hot Chocolate Mix
- 2 teaspoons baking powder
- 1/4 teaspoon salt
- 1/2 cup milk
- 2 tablespoons vegetable oil
- 1 teaspoon vanilla extract
- 1/2 cup packed brown sugar
- 1 and 1/4 cups hot water

Ingredients for the Whipped Cream:

- 1 cup heavy cream
- 2 tablespoons powdered sugar
- 1 teaspoon vanilla extract

Instructions:

1. Preheat your oven to 350°F (175°C) and grease a baking dish.
2. In a medium bowl, whisk together the all-purpose flour, granulated sugar, Medieval Hot Chocolate Mix, baking powder, and salt.
3. Stir in the milk, vegetable oil, and vanilla extract until the batter is smooth.
4. Spread the batter evenly into the prepared baking dish.
5. In a separate bowl, mix the brown sugar and 2 tablespoons of the Medieval Hot Chocolate Mix. Sprinkle this mixture evenly over the batter in the baking dish.
6. Pour the hot water over the top, but do not stir.
7. Bake for 30-35 minutes, or until the top of the pudding is set and the edges are slightly crispy.
8. While the pudding is baking, prepare the whipped cream. In a large bowl, beat the heavy cream, powdered sugar, and vanilla extract until soft peaks form.
9. Serve the Warm Medieval Hot Chocolate Pudding with dollops of whipped cream on top.

§

Warm Medieval Hot Chocolate Rice Pudding with Raisins and Cinnamon

Savor the comforting and rich flavors of this Warm Medieval Hot Chocolate Rice Pudding, where the delicate sweetness of the hot chocolate mix perfectly complements the creamy texture of the rice and the delightful burst of flavor from the raisins, creating a dessert that is perfect for cozy evenings or for sharing with loved ones during special gatherings.

Ingredients:

- 1 cup uncooked white rice
- 2 cups water

- 2 cups milk
- 1/2 cup Medieval Hot Chocolate Mix
- 1/2 cup raisins
- 1/4 teaspoon ground cinnamon
- 1/4 teaspoon salt
- Whipped cream, for serving (optional)

Instructions:

1. In a medium saucepan, combine the white rice, water, and a pinch of salt. Bring to a boil over medium-high heat.
2. Reduce the heat to low, cover the saucepan, and simmer for 15-20 minutes, or until the rice is cooked and the liquid is absorbed.
3. Stir in the milk, Medieval Hot Chocolate Mix, raisins, and ground cinnamon. Cook over low heat, stirring occasionally, for an additional 15-20 minutes, or until the mixture has thickened to a pudding-like consistency.
4. Remove the saucepan from the heat and let the rice pudding cool slightly.
5. Serve the Warm Medieval Hot Chocolate Rice Pudding in individual bowls, garnishing each portion with a sprinkle of ground cinnamon and a dollop of whipped cream if desired.

§

Warm Medieval Hot Chocolate Tarts with Raspberry Jam

Indulge in the delightful warmth of the Warm Medieval Hot Chocolate Tarts with Raspberry Jam, a delectable dessert that combines the rich flavors of the Medieval Hot Chocolate Mix with the vibrant sweetness of raspberry jam, all encased within a delicate and buttery tart shell. As you take your first bite, the crisp and flaky texture of the tart shell gives way to a luxurious, velvety filling, where the decadent essence of the hot chocolate mix shines through, enveloping your taste buds in a comforting embrace of familiar, nostalgic flavors. Each spoonful presents a delightful contrast, with the luscious chocolate filling mingling harmoniously with the bright, fruity notes of the raspberry jam, creating a symphony of tastes that dance on your palate. The delicate sweetness of the jam complements the robust richness of the chocolate, enhancing the overall experience and leaving a lingering sensation that is both satisfying and uplifting.

Enjoy these Warm Medieval Hot Chocolate Tarts with Raspberry Jam as a delightful conclusion to a memorable meal, or as a luxurious treat to share with loved ones during special occasions and gatherings. Let the enchanting combination of flavors transport you to a realm of pure culinary delight, where every bite is a celebration of warmth, comfort, and the joy of savoring life's simple pleasures.

Ingredients:

For the Tart Shells:
- 1 and 1/4 cups all-purpose flour
- 1/2 cup unsalted butter, chilled and cubed
- 2 tablespoons granulated sugar
- 1/4 teaspoon salt
- 1 large egg yolk
- 2 tablespoons ice water

For the Filling:
- 1 cup Medieval Hot Chocolate Mix
- 1 and 1/4 cups heavy cream
- 2 large eggs
- 1 teaspoon vanilla extract

For the Topping:
- 1/2 cup raspberry jam

Instructions:

1. For the Tart Shells: In a food processor, pulse together the flour, butter, sugar, and salt until the mixture resembles coarse crumbs. Add the egg yolk and ice water, and pulse until the dough comes together. Shape the dough into a disc, wrap it in plastic wrap, and refrigerate for 30 minutes.

2. Preheat your oven to 375°F (190°C). On a lightly floured surface, roll out the chilled dough and cut it into circles to fit your tart pans. Press the dough into the pans, prick the bottoms with a fork, and bake for 12-15 minutes, or until the shells are lightly golden. Let them cool completely.

3. For the Filling: In a saucepan, heat the heavy cream until it just begins to simmer. Remove from heat and whisk in the Medieval Hot Chocolate Mix until fully combined. In a separate bowl, whisk the eggs and vanilla extract together, then gradually add the hot chocolate mixture, whisking constantly.

4. Pour the filling into the cooled tart shells and bake for 15-20 minutes, or until the filling is set. Let the tarts cool slightly.

5. Heat the raspberry jam in a small saucepan or in the microwave until it becomes pourable. Drizzle the warm jam over the tarts.

6. Serve the Warm Medieval Hot Chocolate Tarts with Raspberry Jam, savoring the harmonious blend of rich chocolate, delicate pastry, and the fruity sweetness of the raspberry jam, creating a delightful dessert that is perfect for enjoying with friends and loved ones, or as an exquisite treat to elevate any special occasion.

Medieval Hot Chocolate Scented Caramel Apples with Toppings

Savor the delightful Medieval Hot Chocolate Scented Caramel Apples with a variety of toppings, relishing the delightful contrast between the crisp, juicy apples, and the luscious, aromatic caramel infused with the rich flavors of the Medieval Hot Chocolate Mix. These delectable treats are perfect for enjoying on festive occasions, as a special treat for loved ones, or as a delightful way to indulge in the comforting flavors of the season.

Ingredients:

- 6 medium-sized apples
- 1 cup granulated sugar
- 1 cup heavy cream
- 1/4 cup unsalted butter
- 2 tablespoons Medieval Hot Chocolate Mix
- Toppings of your choice (chopped nuts, mini marshmallows, sprinkles, etc.)

Wooden sticks or skewers for dipping

Instructions:

1. Wash and dry the apples thoroughly. Remove the stems and insert the wooden sticks or skewers into the tops.
2. In a heavy-bottomed saucepan, heat the granulated sugar over medium heat, stirring constantly until it melts and turns golden brown.
3. Carefully add the heavy cream and unsalted butter to the caramel, stirring constantly until the mixture is smooth and well combined.
4. Stir in the Medieval Hot Chocolate Mix until fully

incorporated, creating a rich and aromatic chocolate caramel.

5. Dip each apple into the hot caramel, swirling it around to coat the entire surface. Allow any excess caramel to drip off.

6. Immediately roll the caramel-coated apples in your preferred toppings, ensuring they adhere to the surface.

7. Place the coated apples on a parchment-lined baking sheet and let them cool until the caramel sets.

§

Spiced Hot Chocolate Energy Bites with Oats and Almond Butter

Enjoy these Spiced Hot Chocolate Energy Bites with Oats and Almond Butter as a delicious and energizing snack, perfect for satisfying your sweet cravings while providing a wholesome boost of nutrients and the delightful warmth of the Medieval Hot Chocolate Mix. Whether enjoyed as a post-workout treat, an afternoon pick-me-up, or a delightful addition to your on-the-go snack repertoire, these energy bites are sure to keep you fueled and satisfied throughout your day.

Ingredients:

- 1 cup rolled oats
- 1/2 cup almond butter
- 1/3 cup honey
- 2 tablespoons Medieval Hot Chocolate Mix
- 1/4 cup unsweetened shredded coconut, plus more for rolling (optional)
- 1/4 cup mini chocolate chips (optional)
- 1 teaspoon vanilla extract

Instructions:

1. In a large mixing bowl, combine the rolled oats, almond butter, honey, Medieval Hot Chocolate Mix, shredded coconut, chocolate chips, and vanilla extract. Stir until all the ingredients are well combined.
2. Cover the bowl and chill the mixture in the refrigerator for 30 minutes to firm up.
3. Once chilled, use a tablespoon or a small cookie scoop to portion the mixture and roll it into bite-sized balls.
4. If desired, roll the energy bites in additional shredded coconut to coat the exterior.
5. Place the energy bites on a baking sheet lined with parchment paper and refrigerate for at least 1 hour before serving.

§

Spiced Hot Chocolate Energy Bars with Nuts and Dried Fruit

Enjoy these Spiced Hot Chocolate Energy Bars with Nuts and Dried Fruit as a nutritious and satisfying snack, providing a delightful blend of wholesome oats, nuts, and dried fruit, all infused with the comforting and invigorating flavors of the Medieval Hot Chocolate Mix. Whether enjoyed as an on-the-go breakfast option, a midday treat, or a pre-workout boost, these energy bars are sure to keep you energized and ready to tackle the day ahead.

Ingredients:

- 2 cups old-fashioned rolled oats
- 1 cup chopped nuts (almonds, walnuts, or your preferred choice)
- 1/2 cup dried fruit (cranberries, raisins, or chopped dates)

- 1/4 cup Medieval Hot Chocolate Mix
- 1/2 cup almond butter
- 1/3 cup honey
- 1 teaspoon vanilla extract

Instructions:

1. Preheat your oven to 350°F (175°C) and line a baking dish with parchment paper.
2. In a large mixing bowl, combine the rolled oats, chopped nuts, dried fruit, and Medieval Hot Chocolate Mix. Mix well to ensure even distribution of the ingredients.
3. In a separate microwave-safe bowl, combine the almond butter and honey. Microwave the mixture for 30-60 seconds, or until it is easily stirrable. Stir in the vanilla extract.
4. Pour the almond butter mixture over the dry ingredients and mix until everything is evenly coated.
5. Transfer the mixture to the prepared baking dish and press it down firmly into an even layer.
6. Bake for 15-20 minutes, or until the edges are golden brown.
7. Allow the energy bars to cool completely in the baking dish before slicing them into bars or squares.

§

Spiced Hot Chocolate Energy Bars with Quinoa and Avocado

Picture sinking your teeth into a delectable Spiced Hot Chocolate Energy Bar with Quinoa and Avocado, a unique and nutritious treat that combines the wholesome goodness of quinoa and the creamy richness of avocado with the comforting essence of the Medieval Hot Chocolate Mix. With the first bite, the soft and velvety texture of the avocado effortlessly melds with the chewy quinoa, creating a delightful harmony that is further enhanced by the robust flavors of the hot chocolate mix.

The avocado adds a subtle creaminess and a wealth of beneficial nutrients to the energy bar, infusing each bite with a touch of indulgence and a boost of heart-healthy fats. As you savor the intricate blend of flavors and textures, you'll find yourself immersed in a truly satisfying and nourishing experience that invigorates your senses and uplifts your spirit.

Enjoy these Spiced Hot Chocolate Energy Bars with Quinoa and Avocado as a delightful snack that not only satisfies your taste buds but also provides a wholesome and energizing boost, perfect for fueling your day with a blend of natural goodness and the comforting warmth of spiced hot chocolate.

Ingredients:

- 1 cup cooked quinoa
- 1 ripe avocado, mashed
- 1/4 cup Medieval Hot Chocolate Mix
- 1/2 cup almond butter
- 1/3 cup honey
- 1 teaspoon vanilla extract
- 1/2 cup chopped nuts (such as almonds or walnuts)
- 1/4 cup dried cranberries or raisins

Instructions:

1. Preheat your oven to 350°F (175°C) and line a baking dish with parchment paper.
2. In a large mixing bowl, combine the cooked quinoa, mashed avocado, Medieval Hot Chocolate Mix, almond butter, honey, and vanilla extract. Mix well to ensure all

the ingredients are thoroughly incorporated.
3. Fold in the chopped nuts and dried cranberries or raisins.
4. Transfer the mixture to the prepared baking dish and press it down firmly into an even layer.
5. Bake for 15-20 minutes, or until the edges are golden brown.
6. Allow the energy bars to cool completely in the baking dish before slicing them into bars or squares. Enjoy these unique Spiced Hot Chocolate Energy Bars with Quinoa and Avocado, which offer a delightful blend of wholesome quinoa and creamy avocado, combined with the rich and invigorating flavors of the Medieval Hot Chocolate Mix. Whether enjoyed as a satisfying breakfast option, a midday pick-me-up, or a post-workout snack, these energy bars provide a nourishing and delicious way to fuel your day.

§

Spiced Hot Chocolate Energy Balls with Chickpeas and Dates

Imagine delighting in Spiced Hot Chocolate Energy Balls with Chickpeas and Dates, a delightful and nutrient-packed treat that combines the earthy wholesomeness of chickpeas with the natural sweetness of dates, all infused with the rich and invigorating flavors of the Medieval Hot Chocolate Mix. As you take your first bite, the soft and chewy texture of the dates blends seamlessly with the subtle nuttiness of the chickpeas, creating a delightful balance of flavors that is further enhanced by the robust essence of the spiced hot chocolate.

The addition of chickpeas infuses each energy ball with a wealth of plant-based protein and fiber, providing a nourishing and satisfying snack that promotes a lasting sense of fullness and energy. Meanwhile, the naturally sweet dates contribute a delightful touch of caramel-like flavor, complementing the warm and comforting notes of the spiced hot chocolate mix to create a truly indulgent and wholesome treat.

Enjoy these Spiced Hot Chocolate Energy Balls with Chickpeas and Dates as a convenient and satisfying snack option, perfect for providing a natural boost of energy and a delightful burst of flavors, while also delivering a wealth of essential nutrients that nourish your body and uplift your spirit.

Ingredients:

- 1 can (15 ounces) chickpeas, drained and rinsed
- 1 cup pitted dates
- 1/4 cup Medieval Hot Chocolate Mix
- 1/2 cup almond butter
- 1 teaspoon vanilla extract
- 1/4 cup shredded coconut, for rolling (optional)

Instructions:

1. In a food processor, combine the chickpeas, pitted dates, Medieval Hot Chocolate Mix, almond butter, and vanilla extract. Pulse until the mixture is well combined and forms a thick, sticky dough.
2. Roll the dough into bite-sized balls, using your hands to shape them evenly.
3. If desired, roll the energy balls in shredded coconut for an extra layer of texture and flavor.
4. Place the energy balls on a baking sheet lined with parchment paper and refrigerate for at least 30 minutes before serving.

Enjoy these Spiced Hot Chocolate Energy Balls with Chickpeas and Dates as a delightful and convenient snack, providing a unique blend of fiber-rich chickpeas and naturally sweet dates, all infused with the rich and invigorating flavors of the Medieval Hot Chocolate Mix. Whether enjoyed as an on-the-go treat, a post-workout snack, or a wholesome indulgence to satisfy your cravings, these energy balls offer a delicious way to stay energized and nourished throughout your day.

RECIPES FOR SPICY MEDIEVAL CHOCOLATE MIX

Cinnamon and Long Pepper Spiced Hot Chocolate French Toast with Berries

Enjoy the delightful and aromatic flavors of the Cinnamon and Long Pepper Spiced Hot Chocolate French Toast, where the warmth of the Spicy Chocolate Mix adds a tantalizing kick to the classic French toast, while the sweet and tangy berries provide a burst of freshness and natural sweetness. Savor this dish as a delightful breakfast option or as a charming treat for a leisurely brunch or special occasion.

Ingredients:

- 4 slices of thick-cut bread (such as brioche or challah)
- 2 large eggs
- 1/2 cup milk
- 2 tablespoons Spicy Chocolate Mix
- 1/2 teaspoon ground cinnamon
- 1 tablespoon butter or oil, for greasing the pan
- Fresh berries (such as strawberries, blueberries, or raspberries), for serving
- Maple syrup or honey, for drizzling (optional)

Instructions:

1. In a shallow dish, whisk together the eggs, milk, Spicy Chocolate Mix, and ground cinnamon until well combined.
2. Dip each slice of bread into the mixture, allowing it to soak for a few seconds on each side.
3. In a skillet or griddle, melt the butter or heat the oil over medium heat.
4. Place the soaked bread slices in the skillet and cook for 2-3 minutes on each side, or until golden brown and cooked through.
5. Serve the Cinnamon and Long Pepper Spiced Hot

Chocolate French Toast with a handful of fresh berries on top. Drizzle with maple syrup or honey, if desired.

§

Cinnamon and Long Pepper Spiced Hot Chocolate Smoothie with Banana and Almond Milk

Ingredients:

- 1 ripe banana, peeled and sliced
- 2 tablespoons Spicy Chocolate Mix
- 1 cup almond milk
- 1/4 teaspoon ground cinnamon
- 1/2 cup ice cubes
- Whipped cream and additional ground long pepper for garnish (optional)

Instructions:

1. In a blender, combine the sliced banana, Spicy Chocolate Mix, almond milk, ground cinnamon, and ice cubes.
2. Blend on high speed until the mixture is smooth and creamy, and the ice is fully incorporated.
3. Pour the smoothie into a glass and top with a dollop of whipped cream, if desired. Sprinkle a pinch of ground long pepper on top for an added kick.
4. Serve immediately and enjoy the delightful fusion of flavors in this Cinnamon and Long Pepper Spiced Hot Chocolate Smoothie, where the aromatic warmth of the Spicy Chocolate Mix beautifully complements the natural sweetness of the banana and almond milk, creating a luxurious and satisfying beverage that is both indulgent and nourishing.

Cinnamon and Long Pepper Spiced Hot Chocolate Waffles with Berries and Whipped Cream

Ingredients:

For the Waffles:
- 1 ½ cups all-purpose flour
- 2 tablespoons Spicy Chocolate Mix
- 2 teaspoons baking powder
- 1/2 teaspoon baking soda
- 1/4 teaspoon salt
- 1 ¼ cups buttermilk
- 2 large eggs
- 1/3 cup melted butter
- 1 teaspoon vanilla extract

For Serving:
- Fresh mixed berries (such as strawberries, blueberries, and raspberries)
- Whipped cream
- Maple syrup or honey, for drizzling (optional)

Instructions:

1. Preheat your waffle iron according to the manufacturer's instructions.
2. In a large mixing bowl, whisk together the flour, Spicy Chocolate Mix, baking powder, baking soda, and salt.
3. In another bowl, whisk together the buttermilk, eggs, melted butter, and vanilla extract.
4. Pour the wet ingredients into the dry ingredients and stir until just combined.
5. Pour the batter onto the preheated waffle iron and cook according to the manufacturer's instructions, until the waffles are crisp and golden.

6. Serve the waffles with a generous helping of mixed berries and a dollop of whipped cream. Drizzle with maple syrup or honey, if desired.

Enjoy the delightful combination of the warm and aromatic flavors of the Cinnamon and Long Pepper Spiced Hot Chocolate Waffles, complemented by the freshness of the mixed berries and the luscious creaminess of the whipped cream, creating a truly indulgent and satisfying breakfast or brunch treat.

§

Long Pepper and Clove Spiced Hot Chocolate Pancakes with Maple Syrup

Ingredients:

- 1 cup all-purpose flour
- 2 tablespoons Spicy Chocolate Mix
- 2 teaspoons baking powder
- 1/2 teaspoon baking soda
- 1/4 teaspoon salt
- 1 cup buttermilk
- 1 large egg
- 2 tablespoons melted butter
- Maple syrup, for serving

Instructions:

1. In a large mixing bowl, whisk together the flour, Spicy Chocolate Mix, baking powder, baking soda, and salt.
2. In a separate bowl, whisk together the buttermilk, egg, and melted butter.
3. Pour the wet ingredients into the dry ingredients and stir until just combined.

4. Heat a lightly greased griddle or non-stick skillet over medium heat.

5. Pour 1/4 cup of batter onto the griddle for each pancake.

6. Cook until bubbles form on the surface of the pancake, then flip and cook until the other side is golden brown.

7. Serve the Long Pepper and Clove Spiced Hot Chocolate Pancakes with a generous drizzle of maple syrup.

Enjoy the delightful fusion of the aromatic long pepper and clove flavors, combined with the rich and indulgent taste of the Spicy Chocolate Mix, creating a truly satisfying and comforting breakfast treat that is perfect for any morning indulgence.

§

Long Pepper and Nutmeg Spiced Hot Chocolate Pancake Stack with Spiced Syrup

Ingredients:

For the Pancakes:
- 1 cup all-purpose flour
- 2 tablespoons Spicy Chocolate Mix
- 2 teaspoons baking powder
- 1/2 teaspoon baking soda
- 1/4 teaspoon salt
- 1 cup buttermilk
- 1 large egg
- 2 tablespoons melted butter

For the Spiced Syrup:
- 1 cup maple syrup
- 1/2 teaspoon ground long pepper

- 1/4 teaspoon ground nutmeg
- Pinch of ground cloves

Instructions:

For the Pancakes:
1. In a large mixing bowl, whisk together the flour, Spicy Chocolate Mix, baking powder, baking soda, and salt.
2. In a separate bowl, whisk together the buttermilk, egg, and melted butter.
3. Pour the wet ingredients into the dry ingredients and stir until just combined.
4. Heat a lightly greased griddle or non-stick skillet over medium heat.
5. Pour 1/4 cup of batter onto the griddle for each pancake.
6. Cook until bubbles form on the surface of the pancake, then flip and cook until the other side is golden brown.

For the Spiced Syrup:
1. In a small saucepan, warm the maple syrup over low heat.
2. Stir in the ground long pepper, ground nutmeg, and a pinch of ground cloves.
3. Simmer for a few minutes to infuse the flavors.

To Serve:
1. Stack the Long Pepper and Nutmeg Spiced Hot Chocolate Pancakes on a plate.
2. Drizzle the warm Spiced Syrup generously over the pancake stack.

Enjoy the delightful medley of flavors in the Long Pepper and Nutmeg Spiced Hot Chocolate Pancake Stack, enhanced by the aromatic and warming notes of the Spicy Chocolate Mix and the tantalizing spiced syrup, creating a truly indulgent breakfast experience that is both comforting and satisfying.

§

Spicy Medieval Hot Chocolate Scented Oatmeal with Brown Sugar, Nuts, and Avocado

Indulge in a hearty bowl of Spicy Medieval Hot Chocolate Scented Oatmeal with Brown Sugar and Nuts, featuring an unexpected twist with the addition of creamy, ripe avocado. Immerse yourself in the rich and aromatic essence of the Spicy Chocolate Mix, where the warm and inviting flavors of cinnamon, long pepper, and nutmeg merge with the earthy undertones of cocoa, creating a delightful harmony of sweet and spiced notes.

Discover the surprising addition of avocado, which lends a velvety and buttery texture to the oatmeal, elevating the dish with its luscious and creamy consistency. Alongside the crunchy medley of chopped nuts and the caramel-like sweetness of brown sugar, the avocado adds a unique richness and depth to the oatmeal, providing a nourishing and satisfying breakfast option that is both wholesome and indulgent.

Savor the delightful combination of textures and flavors, as the creamy avocado perfectly balances the warm and spicy oatmeal, creating a luxurious and comforting breakfast experience that is sure to delight your senses and leave you feeling nourished and satisfied.

Ingredients:

- 1 cup rolled oats
- 2 cups water
- 2 tablespoons Spicy Chocolate Mix
- 2 tablespoons brown sugar
- 1/4 cup mixed nuts (such as almonds, walnuts, or pecans), chopped
- 1/2 ripe avocado, sliced

Instructions:

1. In a saucepan, bring the water to a boil, then add the rolled oats and reduce the heat to medium.
2. Stir in the Spicy Chocolate Mix and cook the oats according to the package instructions, typically for about 5-7 minutes or until they reach your desired consistency.
3. Once the oats are cooked, stir in the brown sugar until it's fully incorporated.
4. Serve the Spicy Medieval Hot Chocolate Scented Oatmeal in bowls, topped with the chopped mixed nuts and slices of ripe avocado.

Enjoy the rich and aromatic flavors of the Spicy Medieval Hot Chocolate Scented Oatmeal, where the warm spices and cocoa notes perfectly complement the creamy avocado, creating a unique and indulgent breakfast experience that is both comforting and satisfying.

Cinnamon and Clove Spiced Hot Chocolate Mousse with Whipped Cream

Ingredients:

- 1 1/2 cups heavy cream
- 1/2 cup whole milk
- 2 tablespoons Spicy Chocolate Mix
- 4 large egg yolks
- 1/4 cup granulated sugar
- 1 teaspoon vanilla extract
- 1/2 teaspoon ground cinnamon
- 1/4 teaspoon ground cloves
- Whipped cream, for topping
- Ground cinnamon, for garnish

Instructions:

1. In a saucepan, heat the heavy cream and whole milk over medium heat until it begins to simmer. Remove from heat and whisk in the Spicy Chocolate Mix until fully combined. Set aside.
2. In a heatproof bowl, whisk together the egg yolks and granulated sugar until the mixture is pale and slightly thickened.
3. Slowly pour the hot cream mixture into the egg yolk mixture, whisking constantly.
4. Return the mixture to the saucepan and cook over low heat, stirring constantly, until the mixture thickens and coats the back of a spoon. Do not let it boil.
5. Remove from heat and stir in the vanilla extract, ground cinnamon, and ground cloves.
6. Pour the mixture into serving glasses or bowls and refrigerate for at least 2 hours, or until set.
7. Before serving, top the mousse with a dollop of whipped cream and a sprinkle of ground cinnamon.

Enjoy the decadent and luscious Cinnamon and Clove Spiced Hot Chocolate Mousse, where the aromatic spices create a delightful warmth that beautifully complements the rich and velvety texture of the mousse. The luxurious addition of whipped cream adds a light and airy touch, creating a delightful contrast in both texture and flavor. Savor this exquisite dessert as a perfect conclusion to any meal or as a standalone indulgence that is sure to captivate your taste buds.

§

Cinnamon and Clove Spiced Hot Chocolate Muffins with a Cocoa Drizzle

Enjoy the delightful aroma and rich flavors of the Cinnamon and Clove Spiced Hot Chocolate Muffins, where the blend of warm spices and cocoa creates a comforting and indulgent treat. The addition of the decadent Cocoa Drizzle adds an extra layer of chocolatey goodness, making these muffins a perfect accompaniment to your morning coffee or an afternoon tea.

Ingredients:

For the Muffins:
- 1 ¾ cups all-purpose flour
- 1/2 cup unsweetened cocoa powder
- 1 tablespoon Spicy Chocolate Mix
- 2 teaspoons baking powder
- 1/2 teaspoon baking soda
- 1/4 teaspoon salt
- 1 teaspoon ground cinnamon
- 1/4 teaspoon ground cloves
- 1/2 cup granulated sugar

- 1 cup milk
- 1/3 cup vegetable oil

- 1 large egg
- 1 teaspoon vanilla extract

For the Cocoa Drizzle:
- 1/2 cup powdered sugar
- 2 tablespoons unsweetened cocoa powder
- 2-3 tablespoons milk

Instructions:

1. Preheat the oven to 375°F (190°C). Line a muffin tin with paper liners or grease with cooking spray.
2. In a large bowl, whisk together the flour, cocoa powder, Spicy Chocolate Mix, baking powder, baking soda, salt, ground cinnamon, and ground cloves.
3. In another bowl, whisk together the sugar, milk, vegetable oil, egg, and vanilla extract until well combined.
4. Pour the wet ingredients into the dry ingredients and stir until just combined.
5. Divide the batter evenly among the muffin cups, filling each about 2/3 full.
6. Bake for 18-20 minutes, or until a toothpick inserted into the center of a muffin comes out clean.
7. While the muffins cool, prepare the Cocoa Drizzle. In a small bowl, whisk together the powdered sugar, cocoa powder, and milk until smooth.
8. Drizzle the Cocoa Drizzle over the cooled muffins.

Cinnamon and Long Pepper Spiced Hot Chocolate Cheesecake with Chocolate Ganache

Enjoy the rich and aromatic flavors of the Cinnamon and Long Pepper Spiced Hot Chocolate Cheesecake, where the velvety texture of the cheesecake perfectly balances the warm and spicy notes of the Spicy Chocolate Mix, all beautifully complemented by the luxurious and decadent chocolate ganache topping. Savor this exquisite dessert as a perfect finale to any meal or as a delightful treat for any special occasion.

Ingredients:

For the Crust:
- 1 1/2 cups graham cracker crumbs
- 1/4 cup granulated sugar
- 1/2 cup unsalted butter, melted

For the Cheesecake Filling:
- 24 ounces (680g) cream cheese, softened
- 1 cup granulated sugar
- 2 tablespoons all-purpose flour
- 3 large eggs
- 1 cup sour cream
- 1/4 cup heavy cream
- 2 tablespoons Spicy Chocolate Mix (1 cup unsweetened cocoa powder, 1 cup granulated sugar, 1 teaspoon ground cinnamon, 3/4 teaspoon ground long pepper, 1/4 teaspoon ground nutmeg, pinch of ground cloves)

For the Chocolate Ganache:
- 1/2 cup heavy cream
- 1 cup semisweet chocolate chips
- 1 tablespoon unsalted butter

Instructions:

For the Crust:

1. Preheat the oven to 325°F (165°C). Grease a 9-inch springform pan.
2. In a medium bowl, combine the graham cracker crumbs, sugar, and melted butter. Press the mixture

firmly into the bottom of the prepared pan.
3. Bake the crust for 10 minutes, then set aside to cool.

For the Cheesecake Filling:

1. In a large bowl, beat the cream cheese and sugar until smooth. Add the flour and mix until combined.
2. Beat in the eggs, one at a time, then add the sour cream and heavy cream. Mix until the batter is smooth and creamy.
3. Stir in the Spicy Chocolate Mix until fully incorporated.
4. Pour the filling over the cooled crust and smooth the top with a spatula.
5. Bake the cheesecake for 45-50 minutes, or until the edges are set and the center is slightly jiggly.
6. Turn off the oven and let the cheesecake cool in the oven with the door slightly ajar for 1 hour.
7. Remove the cheesecake from the oven and let it cool completely. Refrigerate for at least 4 hours or overnight.

For the Chocolate Ganache:

1. In a small saucepan, heat the heavy cream over medium heat until it begins to simmer.
2. Place the chocolate chips in a heatproof bowl and pour the hot cream over the chocolate. Let it sit for 1 minute, then stir until the chocolate is completely melted and the mixture is smooth.
3. Stir in the butter until it's fully incorporated.
4. Let the ganache cool for 10-15 minutes, then pour it

over the chilled cheesecake.
5. Refrigerate the cheesecake for an additional 30
minutes to set the ganache.

§

Cinnamon and Long Pepper Spiced Hot Chocolate Donuts with Sugar Glaze

Enjoy the delightful aroma and rich flavors of the Cinnamon and Long Pepper Spiced Hot Chocolate Donuts, where the warm spices and cocoa create a comforting and indulgent treat. The sweet and simple sugar glaze adds a touch of sweetness and a satisfying finish, making these donuts a perfect accompaniment to your morning coffee or a delightful treat for any time of day.

Ingredients:

For the Donuts:

- 2 cups all-purpose flour
- 1/2 cup granulated sugar
- 1/4 cup unsweetened cocoa powder
- 2 tablespoons Spicy Chocolate Mix
- 2 teaspoons baking powder
- 1/2 teaspoon baking soda
- 1/2 teaspoon ground cinnamon
- 1/4 teaspoon ground long pepper
- 1/4 teaspoon salt
- 1 cup buttermilk
- 2 large eggs
- 2 tablespoons unsalted butter, melted and cooled
- 1 teaspoon vanilla extract

For the Sugar Glaze:

- 1 1/2 cups powdered sugar
- 3-4 tablespoons milk
- 1 teaspoon vanilla extract

Instructions:

For the Donuts:

1. Preheat your oven to 350°F (175°C). Grease a donut pan with non-stick cooking spray.
2. In a large bowl, whisk together the flour, sugar, cocoa powder, Spicy Chocolate Mix, baking powder, baking soda, ground cinnamon, ground long pepper, and salt.
3. In another bowl, whisk together the buttermilk, eggs, melted butter, and vanilla extract until well combined.
4. Pour the wet ingredients into the dry ingredients and stir until just combined.
5. Spoon the batter into a piping bag or a large zip-top bag with the corner snipped off.
6. Pipe the batter into the prepared donut pan, filling each cavity about 2/3 full.
7. Bake for 12-14 minutes, or until a toothpick inserted into the donuts comes out clean.
8. Remove the donuts from the oven and let them cool in the pan for a few minutes before transferring them to a wire rack to cool completely.

For the Sugar Glaze:

1. In a medium bowl, whisk together the powdered sugar, milk, and vanilla extract until smooth. Adjust the consistency by adding more milk if needed.
2. Dip each cooled donut into the sugar glaze, then return them to the wire rack to set.

Cinnamon and Long Pepper Spiced Hot Chocolate French Toast Roll-Ups with Homemade Hazelnut Spread

Enjoy the delightful combination of warm and spicy flavors in the Cinnamon and Long Pepper Spiced Hot Chocolate French Toast Roll-Ups, complemented by the creamy and indulgent homemade hazelnut spread. These roll-ups make for a delightful and satisfying breakfast or brunch treat that is sure to be a hit with the whole family.

Ingredients:

For the French Toast Roll-Ups:

- 8 slices of white or whole wheat bread, crusts removed
- 2 large eggs
- 1/2 cup milk
- 1 teaspoon vanilla extract
- 2 tablespoons Spicy Chocolate Mix
- 1/4 teaspoon ground cinnamon
- 1/4 teaspoon ground long pepper
- 2 tablespoons unsalted butter, melted
- Powdered sugar, for dusting (optional)

For the Homemade Hazelnut Spread:

- 1 cup roasted hazelnuts
- 2 tablespoons unsweetened cocoa powder
- 3 tablespoons powdered sugar
- 2 tablespoons vegetable oil
- 1/2 teaspoon vanilla extract
- Pinch of salt

Instructions:

For the Homemade Hazelnut Spread:

1. In a food processor, blend the roasted hazelnuts until they form a smooth paste.
2. Add the cocoa powder, powdered sugar, vegetable oil, vanilla extract, and a pinch of salt. Blend until well combined and creamy. Set aside.

For the French Toast Roll-Ups:

1. In a shallow dish, whisk together the eggs, milk, vanilla extract, Spicy Chocolate Mix, ground cinnamon, and ground long pepper until well combined.
2. Use a rolling pin to flatten each slice of bread.
3. Spread a generous amount of the homemade hazelnut spread onto each flattened slice of bread.
4. Roll up the bread tightly and dip each roll-up into the egg mixture, coating all sides.
5. In a large skillet or griddle, heat the melted butter over medium heat.
6. Cook the French toast roll-ups for 2-3 minutes per side, or until they are golden brown and crispy.
7. Remove the roll-ups from the skillet and let them cool slightly before dusting with powdered sugar, if desired.

Indulge in the rich and decadent flavors of the Long Pepper and Cinnamon Spiced Hot Chocolate Brownies, where the aromatic blend of long pepper and cinnamon beautifully complements the deep and luscious essence of hot chocolate. This delightful treat combines the comforting familiarity of traditional brownies with an added touch of warmth and spice, creating an irresistible symphony of flavors that is sure to tantalize your taste buds and leave you longing for more.

Long Pepper and Cinnamon Spiced Hot Chocolate Brownies

Each bite of these brownies offers a perfect balance of velvety texture and fudgy richness, enhanced by the nuanced notes of long pepper and cinnamon that delicately dance on your palate. The carefully curated Spicy Chocolate Mix, with its hints of cocoa, cinnamon, and a touch of long pepper, adds a unique and sophisticated twist to the classic brownie, elevating it to a whole new level of indulgence.

As you take in the aroma of freshly baked brownies wafting through the air, you'll be drawn in by the tantalizing blend of fragrant spices and rich chocolate, creating an alluring sensory experience that awakens the senses and evokes a sense of comfort and warmth. These brownies are perfect for any occasion, whether you're enjoying a quiet evening at home or sharing a delightful treat with friends and loved ones.

With their irresistible aroma, delectable taste, and charming blend of spices, the Long Pepper and Cinnamon Spiced Hot Chocolate Brownies are a delightful indulgence that promises to delight even the most discerning of palates. Enjoy them with a warm cup of coffee or a refreshing glass of milk for the ultimate treat that will leave you with a lasting impression of comfort and satisfaction.

Ingredients:

- 1 cup unsalted butter
- 2 cups granulated sugar
- 4 large eggs
- 1 teaspoon vanilla extract
- 1 cup all-purpose flour

- 3/4 cup Spicy Chocolate Mix
- 1/4 teaspoon salt
- 1/2 cup semisweet chocolate chips

Instructions:

1. Preheat your oven to 350°F (175°C). Grease a 9x13 inch baking pan and line it with parchment paper.
2. In a medium saucepan, melt the butter over low heat. Remove from heat and stir in the sugar until well combined.
3. Beat in the eggs, one at a time, and then stir in the vanilla extract.
4. In a separate bowl, whisk together the flour, Spicy Chocolate Mix, and salt.
5. Gradually add the dry ingredients to the wet ingredients, mixing until just combined. Be careful not to overmix.
6. Fold in the chocolate chips.
7. Pour the batter into the prepared baking pan and smooth the top with a spatula.
8. Bake for 25-30 minutes, or until a toothpick inserted into the center comes out with a few moist crumbs.
9. Allow the brownies to cool completely in the pan before slicing and serving.

§

Long Pepper and Clove Spiced Hot Chocolate Whoopie Pies with Marshmallow Filling

Indulge in the irresistible allure of the Long Pepper and Clove Spiced Hot Chocolate Whoopie Pies with Marshmallow Filling, where the aromatic blend of warm spices, including long pepper and cloves, beautifully harmonizes with the rich and comforting essence of hot chocolate. These delightful treats boast a soft and cakey texture, perfectly sandwiched together with a luscious layer of marshmallow filling, creating a symphony of flavors and textures that is sure to captivate your taste buds and leave you yearning for more.

With every bite, savor the nuanced notes of the carefully curated spice blend, where the subtle heat of the long pepper mingles with the fragrant and aromatic essence of cloves, perfectly balanced by the delicate sweetness of the marshmallow filling. The velvety smoothness of the chocolate-infused cake envelops your senses, offering a moment of pure indulgence and comfort that transports you to a world of rich and decadent flavors.

These delectable whoopie pies are a delightful addition to any gathering or celebration, offering a unique twist on a beloved classic that is sure to delight guests and loved ones alike. Share these irresistible treats with friends over a warm cup of coffee or present them as a sweet finale to a memorable meal, and let the comforting and aromatic blend of long pepper and cloves elevate your dessert experience to new heights.

Ingredients:

For the Whoopie Pies:
- 2 cups all-purpose flour
- 1/2 cup unsweetened cocoa powder
- 1 teaspoon baking powder
- 1/2 teaspoon baking soda
- 1/2 teaspoon ground long pepper
- 1/2 teaspoon ground cloves
- 1/2 teaspoon Spicy Chocolate Mix

- 1/4 teaspoon salt
- 1/2 cup unsalted butter, softened
- 1 cup granulated sugar
- 1 large egg
- 1 teaspoon vanilla extract
- 1 cup buttermilk

For the Marshmallow Filling:
- 1/2 cup unsalted butter, softened
- 1 cup confectioners' sugar
- 1 cup marshmallow fluff
- 1 teaspoon vanilla extract

Instructions:

For the Whoopie Pies:
1. Preheat your oven to 350°F (175°C). Line a baking sheet with parchment paper.
2. In a medium bowl, sift together the flour, cocoa powder, baking powder, baking soda, ground long pepper, ground cloves, Spicy Chocolate Mix, and salt.
3. In a large bowl, cream together the butter and sugar until light and fluffy. Beat in the egg and vanilla extract.
4. Gradually add the dry ingredients to the wet ingredients, alternating with the buttermilk, beginning and ending with the dry ingredients. Mix until just combined.
5. Drop rounded tablespoons of batter onto the prepared baking sheet, spacing them about 2 inches apart.
6. Bake for 10-12 minutes, or until the tops spring back when lightly touched. Let the pies cool completely on a wire rack.

For the Marshmallow Filling:
1. In a medium bowl, beat the softened butter and confectioners' sugar until light and fluffy.

2. Add the marshmallow fluff and vanilla extract, and continue beating until the filling is smooth and well combined.

To Assemble:
1. Spread a generous amount of the marshmallow filling onto the flat side of half of the cooled whoopie pies.
2. Top with the remaining whoopie pies to create delightful sandwich cookies.

§

Long Pepper and Nutmeg Spiced Hot Chocolate Caramel Popcorn

Enjoy the delightful combination of warming spices in the Long Pepper and Nutmeg Spiced Hot Chocolate Caramel Popcorn, where the aromatic blend of the Spicy Chocolate Mix complements the sweet and buttery caramel coating, creating a satisfying treat that is perfect for enjoying during movie nights, gatherings, or any time you're craving a delectable and comforting snack.

Ingredients:

- 12 cups popped popcorn
- 1 cup unsalted butter
- 1 cup packed brown sugar
- 1/2 cup light corn syrup
- 1/2 teaspoon salt
- 1/2 teaspoon Spicy Chocolate Mix
- 1/2 teaspoon ground nutmeg
- 1/2 teaspoon vanilla extract
- 1/4 teaspoon baking soda

Instructions:

1. Preheat your oven to 250°F (120°C). Line a baking sheet with parchment paper or a silicone baking mat.
2. Place the popped popcorn in a large bowl and set aside.
3. In a medium saucepan over medium heat, melt the butter. Stir in the brown sugar, corn syrup, salt, Spicy Chocolate Mix, ground nutmeg, and ground long pepper. Bring the mixture to a boil, stirring constantly.
4. Allow the mixture to boil without stirring for 4 minutes. Remove from heat and stir in the vanilla extract and baking soda. The mixture will foam up slightly.
5. Pour the caramel mixture over the popcorn and stir until the popcorn is evenly coated.
6. Spread the coated popcorn onto the prepared baking sheet.
7. Bake for 1 hour, stirring every 15 minutes.
8. Allow the caramel popcorn to cool completely before breaking it into pieces and serving.

§

Long Pepper and Nutmeg Spiced Hot Chocolate Granola with Dried Fruits and Nuts

Enjoy the delightful blend of warm spices in the Long Pepper and Nutmeg Spiced Hot Chocolate Granola, enhanced by the aromatic touch of the Spicy Chocolate Mix, along with the delightful combination of dried fruits and nuts. This flavorful and wholesome granola makes for a perfect breakfast or snack, offering a satisfying and indulgent treat that is sure to brighten up your day.

Ingredients:

- 3 cups old-fashioned rolled oats
- 1 cup mixed nuts (such as almonds, walnuts, and pecans), chopped
- 1/2 cup mixed dried fruits (such as cranberries, raisins, and apricots), chopped
- 1/4 cup unsweetened shredded coconut
- 1/4 cup honey
- 1/4 cup melted coconut oil
- 1/4 cup Spicy Chocolate Mix
- 1 teaspoon ground nutmeg
- 1/4 teaspoon salt
- 1 teaspoon vanilla extract

Instructions:

1. Preheat your oven to 300°F (150°C). Line a baking sheet with parchment paper.
2. In a large bowl, combine the rolled oats, mixed nuts, mixed dried fruits, and shredded coconut.
3. In a separate bowl, whisk together the honey, melted coconut oil, Spicy Chocolate Mix, ground nutmeg, salt, and vanilla extract until well combined.
4. Pour the wet ingredients over the dry ingredients and mix until the oats and nuts are evenly coated.
5. Spread the mixture evenly on the prepared baking sheet.
6. Bake for 25-30 minutes, or until the granola is golden brown and fragrant, stirring halfway through.
7. Allow the granola to cool completely on the baking sheet before transferring it to an airtight container for storage.

Long Pepper and Nutmeg Spiced Hot Chocolate Milkshake

This delightful milkshake is the perfect treat for any occasion, offering a delightful blend of warm spices and rich chocolate, all beautifully enhanced by the aromatic touch of the Spicy Chocolate Mix. Enjoy the satisfying and comforting flavors of this milkshake as a refreshing and indulgent dessert that is sure to delight your taste buds and leave you feeling content and satisfied.

Ingredients:

- 2 cups vanilla ice cream
- 1 cup milk
- 1/4 cup Spicy Chocolate Mix (1 cup unsweetened cocoa powder, 1 cup granulated sugar, 1 teaspoon ground cinnamon, 1/2 teaspoon ground long pepper, pinch of ground cloves)
- 1/2 teaspoon ground nutmeg
- Whipped cream, for garnish
- Grated chocolate, for garnish
- Long pepper, for garnish

Instructions:

1. In a blender, combine the vanilla ice cream, milk, Spicy Chocolate Mix, and ground nutmeg.
2. Blend until smooth and creamy, adjusting the consistency with more milk if needed.
3. Pour the milkshake into glasses.
4. Top with whipped cream and grated chocolate.
5. Sprinkle a pinch of ground long pepper on top for an extra kick of warmth and spice.
6. Serve immediately and enjoy the rich and indulgent flavors of the Long Pepper and Nutmeg Spiced Hot Chocolate Milkshake.

Long Pepper and Nutmeg Spiced Hot Chocolate Pudding with Vanilla Custard

During medieval times, the art of culinary refinement had begun to evolve, giving rise to a diverse range of dishes that showcased a blend of distinct flavors and exotic ingredients. Dishes such as the Long Pepper and Nutmeg Spiced Hot Chocolate Pudding with Vanilla Custard would have been considered a luxurious indulgence, appreciated for its rich, aromatic flavors and the meticulous effort required for its preparation.

In the medieval context, the use of spices, including long pepper and nutmeg, was highly esteemed and often associated with wealth and sophistication. The inclusion of these spices in the hot chocolate pudding would have imparted a sense of exoticism and opulence, captivating the senses with their warm and fragrant notes, reminiscent of distant lands and thriving trade routes.

Accompanying the rich and spiced hot chocolate pudding, the smooth and velvety vanilla custard would have provided a delightful contrast, offering a touch of sweetness and a soothing counterbalance to the intricate blend of flavors. The delicate aroma of vanilla would have added a layer of refinement to the dish, enhancing its overall appeal and contributing to its status as a sought-after delicacy among the nobility and aristocracy.

Overall, the Long Pepper and Nutmeg Spiced Hot Chocolate Pudding with Vanilla Custard represents the culinary artistry of the medieval era, showcasing a harmonious fusion of diverse ingredients and flavors that symbolized not only gastronomic sophistication but also the cultural exchange and exploration of new culinary horizons during that fascinating period in history.

Ingredients for the Pudding:

- 1/2 cup granulated sugar
- 1/4 cup unsweetened cocoa powder
- 1/4 cup Spicy Chocolate Mix
- 3 tablespoons cornstarch
- 1/4 teaspoon ground nutmeg
- 1/4 teaspoon salt
- 2 1/4 cups whole milk
- 2 tablespoons unsalted butter
- 1 teaspoon vanilla extract

Ingredients for the Vanilla Custard:

- 2 cups whole milk
- 1/4 cup granulated sugar
- 3 large egg yolks
- 2 tablespoons cornstarch
- 1 teaspoon vanilla extract

Instructions:

For the Pudding:

1. In a medium saucepan, whisk together the sugar, cocoa powder, Spicy Chocolate Mix, cornstarch, ground nutmeg, and salt.
2. Gradually whisk in the whole milk until the mixture is smooth.
3. Cook over medium heat, stirring constantly, until the pudding thickens and comes to a boil.
4. Remove from heat and stir in the butter and vanilla extract until the butter is fully melted and incorporated.
5. Pour the pudding into individual serving dishes or

a large bowl. Cover with plastic wrap, making sure the plastic wrap touches the surface of the pudding to prevent a skin from forming. Refrigerate for at least 2 hours.

For the Vanilla Custard:

1. In a saucepan, heat the milk over medium heat until it begins to simmer.
2. In a separate bowl, whisk together the sugar, egg yolks, and cornstarch until well combined and slightly pale.
3. Slowly pour the hot milk into the egg mixture, whisking constantly.
4. Pour the mixture back into the saucepan and cook over medium heat, stirring constantly, until it thickens.
5. Remove from heat and stir in the vanilla extract.
6. Pour the custard into a bowl and cover with plastic wrap, making sure the plastic wrap touches the surface of the custard to prevent a skin from forming. Refrigerate until ready to serve.

To Serve:

1. Spoon the chilled Long Pepper and Nutmeg Spiced Hot Chocolate Pudding into serving dishes.
2. Top with the chilled Vanilla Custard.
3. Serve chilled and enjoy the delightful combination of warm spices and rich chocolate, beautifully complemented by the smooth and creamy Vanilla Custard.

This Long Pepper and Nutmeg Spiced Hot Chocolate Pudding with Vanilla Custard is a delightful and indulgent dessert that is perfect for special occasions or whenever you're craving a rich and comforting treat.

Spicy Hot Chocolate Biscuit Cake with Layers of Cream and Berries

A biscuit cake is a dessert made by layering tea biscuits or cookies with various fillings, often cream, frosting, or fruits, and allowing it to set in a refrigerator until the layers bind together to form a cohesive cake-like structure. The biscuits absorb the moisture from the cream or frosting, resulting in a cake-like texture that doesn't require baking.

The origins of the biscuit cake are believed to date back to the early 20th century, with its popularity growing during times when ingredients like eggs and butter were scarce. This no-bake dessert became a creative solution for producing a delicious and satisfying cake without the need for an oven. It quickly gained popularity for its simplicity, convenience, and versatility, making it an accessible treat for households of all economic backgrounds.

Biscuit cakes have been adapted and modified across various cultures, taking on different forms and flavors based on regional preferences and available ingredients. They have become a staple in many countries, appreciated for their ease of preparation and the endless possibilities for customization, allowing for a wide range of delicious variations. Whether enjoyed as a delectable dessert or a sweet snack, the biscuit cake continues to hold a special place in the hearts of dessert enthusiasts worldwide.

Ingredients:

- 3 cups Spicy Chocolate Mix
- 2 cups heavy cream
- 1/2 cup powdered sugar

- 1 teaspoon vanilla extract
- 2 cups mixed berries (such as strawberries, raspberries, and blueberries)
- 2 packages tea biscuits or graham crackers

Instructions:

1. In a medium bowl, whip the heavy cream until soft peaks form. Add the powdered sugar and vanilla extract, and continue to whip until stiff peaks form. Set aside.

2. Dip the tea biscuits or graham crackers into the Spicy Chocolate Mix, coating each one thoroughly.

3. In a rectangular baking dish, arrange a layer of the chocolate-coated biscuits or graham crackers.

4. Spread a layer of the whipped cream over the biscuits, ensuring an even coverage.

5. Scatter a generous amount of the mixed berries over the cream layer.

6. Repeat the process, creating additional layers of the chocolate-coated biscuits or graham crackers, whipped cream, and mixed berries until you reach the desired number of layers, finishing with a final layer of whipped cream and berries on top.

7. Refrigerate the cake for at least 4 hours, allowing the layers to set and the flavors to meld together.

8. Serve chilled, slicing the Spicy Hot Chocolate Biscuit Cake into portions and savoring the delightful medley of flavors and textures.

Enjoy the sumptuous combination of the aromatic Spicy Chocolate Mix, luscious layers of cream, and vibrant bursts of mixed berries in this delightful cake, which is perfect for any occasion or as a sweet treat to enjoy with family and friends.

§

Spicy Hot Chocolate Chia Seed Pudding with Coconut Milk and Maple Syrup

This delightful and wholesome pudding is perfect for breakfast, dessert, or as a satisfying snack, offering a delightful blend of flavors and textures that are sure to please your palate and leave you feeling nourished and content.

Ingredients:

- 1/2 cup chia seeds
- 2 cups coconut milk
- 1/4 cup Spicy Chocolate Mix
- 2 tablespoons maple syrup
- 1/2 teaspoon vanilla extract
- Shredded coconut and shaved dark chocolate, for garnish

Instructions:

1. In a large bowl, combine the chia seeds, coconut milk, Spicy Chocolate Mix, maple syrup, and vanilla extract. Whisk until well combined.

2. Cover the bowl and refrigerate for at least 4 hours or overnight, allowing the chia seeds to absorb the liquid and create a pudding-like consistency.
3. Before serving, stir the chia seed pudding to ensure an even distribution of the ingredients.

4. Divide the pudding into individual serving dishes or glasses.

5. Garnish with a sprinkle of shredded coconut and shaved dark chocolate.

6. Serve chilled and enjoy the delightful combination of the spicy chocolate flavors, the creamy richness of the coconut milk, and the natural sweetness of the maple syrup in this satisfying and nourishing Spicy Hot Chocolate Chia Seed Pudding.

§

Spicy Medieval Hot Chocolate Flavored Churros with Cinnamon Sugar & Cardamom

These tantalizing churros offer a unique twist on the traditional treat, infusing it with the exotic flavors of the Spicy Chocolate Mix and the distinctive aroma of ground cardamom, resulting in a delightful fusion of medieval-inspired flavors that are sure to captivate your taste buds and transport you to a bygone era of culinary exploration and innovation.

Ingredients:

For the Churros:

- 1 cup water
- 2 tablespoons unsalted butter
- 1 tablespoon granulated sugar
- 1/4 teaspoon salt
- 1 cup all-purpose flour
- 2 eggs
- 1/4 cup Spicy Chocolate Mix

- 1/4 teaspoon ground cardamom
- Vegetable oil, for frying

For the Cinnamon Sugar Coating:

- 1/2 cup granulated sugar
- 1 tablespoon ground cinnamon

Instructions:

1. In a saucepan, combine the water, butter, sugar, and salt, and bring to a boil.

2. Remove the saucepan from the heat and add the flour, Spicy Chocolate Mix, and ground cardamom. Stir vigorously until the mixture forms a ball.

3. Transfer the dough to a piping bag fitted with a large star tip.

4. Heat the vegetable oil in a large pan over medium heat.

5. Pipe the dough directly into the hot oil, using a knife to cut the churros to the desired length.

6. Fry the churros until golden brown, then transfer them to a plate lined with paper towels to drain any excess oil.

7. In a separate bowl, mix the granulated sugar and ground cinnamon for the coating.

8. Roll the warm churros in the cinnamon sugar mixture until evenly coated.

9. Serve the Spicy Medieval Hot Chocolate Flavored Churros with Cinnamon Sugar immediately and enjoy the delightful combination of warm spices,

rich chocolate, and the unexpected hint of aromatic cardamom.

§

Spicy Medieval Hot Chocolate Flavored Rice Pudding with Raisins and Cinnamon

This Spicy Medieval Hot Chocolate Flavored Rice Pudding with Raisins and Cinnamon offers a delightful fusion of flavors and textures, combining the rich and aromatic essence of the Spicy Chocolate Mix with the sweetness of the raisins and the earthy notes of the cinnamon. Enjoy this comforting and indulgent rice pudding as a delightful treat for any occasion, inviting you to savor every spoonful and revel in its rich and satisfying taste.

Ingredients:

- 1 cup Arborio rice
- 2 cups water
- 2 cups milk
- 1/4 cup Spicy Chocolate Mix
- 1/4 teaspoon ground cinnamon
- 1/2 cup raisins
- 1/4 cup honey or maple syrup (for sweetness, if desired)
- 1/4 cup chopped dried figs or dates
- 1/4 cup chopped almonds or pecans (optional, for added texture and crunch)
- Pinch of salt

Instructions:

1. In a large saucepan, bring the water to a boil. Add the rice and a pinch of salt, and simmer for 15 minutes or until the rice is cooked and the water is absorbed.

2. Add the milk, Spicy Chocolate Mix, ground cinnamon, and raisins to the saucepan. Stir well and simmer for an additional 15-20 minutes, or until the mixture thickens to a creamy consistency.

3. Add the honey or maple syrup, adjusting the sweetness to your taste.

4. Stir in the chopped dried figs or dates and the chopped almonds or pecans (if using).

5. Remove the rice pudding from the heat and let it cool for a few minutes.

6. Serve the Spicy Medieval Hot Chocolate Flavored Rice Pudding with Raisins and Cinnamon warm, sprinkled with an extra dash of ground cinnamon for garnish, and enjoy the comforting blend of warm spices, rich chocolate, and the natural sweetness of the fruits in this delightful dessert.

§

Spicy Medieval Hot Chocolate Flavored Thumbprint Cookies with Raspberry Jam

Thumbprint cookies have a rich history that traces back to the early 20th century in Sweden. These delightful cookies are characterized by their small, round shape and their unique indentation, traditionally made by pressing a thumb into the center of the dough before baking. The indentation is then often filled with jam, chocolate, or other sweet fillings, adding a burst of flavor and color to the cookie.

In a medieval-themed cookbook, thumbprint cookies can be a charming addition, representing a bridge between past and present culinary traditions. While thumbprint cookies themselves might not have originated during the medieval era, the concept of small, handcrafted treats with fillings resonates with the essence of traditional medieval desserts.

Within the context of a medieval-themed cookbook, thumbprint cookies can be adapted to incorporate flavors and ingredients that were commonly used during the medieval period, such as spices like cinnamon, nutmeg, and cloves, which were highly valued for their exotic flavors and medicinal properties. Additionally, the use of ingredients like raspberry jam can reflect the appreciation for the natural sweetness of fruits, a characteristic that was prominent in medieval culinary practices.

By infusing thumbprint cookies with the essence of medieval flavors and ingredients, a cookbook can evoke a sense of nostalgia and offer readers a delightful exploration of how contemporary treats can be inspired by the culinary traditions of the past. This approach allows for the celebration of historical influences while presenting a modern twist on classic recipes, fostering a connection between the rich heritage of medieval cuisine and the creative innovations of today's culinary world.

Ingredients:

- 1 cup unsalted butter, softened
- 1/2 cup granulated sugar
- 2 cups all-purpose flour
- 1/4 cup Spicy Chocolate Mix
- 1/4 teaspoon salt
- 1 teaspoon vanilla extract
- 1/2 cup raspberry jam

Instructions:

1. Preheat the oven to 350°F (175°C). Line a baking sheet with parchment paper.

2. In a large mixing bowl, cream together the softened butter and granulated sugar until light and fluffy.

3. Gradually add the flour, Spicy Chocolate Mix, salt, and vanilla extract to the creamed mixture, and mix until a soft dough forms.

4. Shape the dough into 1-inch balls and place them on the prepared baking sheet.

5. Use your thumb or the back of a spoon to make an indentation in the center of each cookie.

6. Fill each indentation with raspberry jam.

7. Bake the cookies for 12-15 minutes, or until the edges are lightly golden.

8. Remove the cookies from the oven and let them cool on the baking sheet for a few minutes before transferring them to a wire rack to cool completely.

9. Serve the Spicy Medieval Hot Chocolate Flavored Thumbprint Cookies with Raspberry Jam as a delightful accompaniment to your favorite hot beverage, and enjoy the delectable blend of rich chocolate, warm spices, and the vibrant sweetness of the raspberry jam in every bite.

These Spicy Medieval Hot Chocolate Flavored Thumbprint Cookies with Raspberry Jam offer a delightful combination of rich flavors and delightful textures, making them the perfect treat for sharing with loved ones or savoring as a comforting indulgence during quiet moments of relaxation.

Spicy Medieval Hot Chocolate Flavored Tiramisu with Cocoa and Mascarpone

In the context of a medieval-themed cookbook, Mascarpone, a creamy, rich, Italian cheese, could be seen as an ingredient that embodies the essence of indulgence and luxury. While not originating from the medieval era, the concept of rich, luxurious dairy products was not entirely foreign to medieval culinary practices.

Mascarpone can be associated with the historical appreciation for delicacies and the availability of fine ingredients that were relished by nobility and the upper echelons of medieval society. Its velvety texture and subtle sweetness could easily symbolize the pursuit of refined taste and opulent dining experiences that were enjoyed by royalty and aristocrats during medieval times.

Incorporating Mascarpone into a recipe such as the Spicy Medieval Hot Chocolate Flavored Tiramisu with Cocoa and Mascarpone serves to elevate the dish to a level of sophistication, while also paying homage to the historical influence of rich and luxurious ingredients that were relished by the privileged few during the medieval period. Its inclusion in a medieval-themed cookbook showcases the crossroads of culinary history and modern interpretation, offering readers a taste of the exquisite flavors and culinary refinements that defined the medieval dining experience, while presenting them in a contemporary and accessible context.

The inclusion of this recipe for Tiramisu offers a fascinating exploration of the evolution of culinary traditions and the adaptation of historical flavors into contemporary dishes. Tiramisu, a popular Italian dessert, represents a fascinating link between the rich culinary heritage of Italy and the exploration of flavors that were enjoyed during the medieval era.

While Tiramisu itself did not originate in the medieval period, its incorporation into a medieval-themed cookbook can symbolize the continuation of culinary practices over time, showcasing how the essence of traditional medieval flavors can be infused into modern interpretations of classic recipes. The layers of flavors and textures in Tiramisu reflect the intricate and layered nature of medieval culinary creations, providing readers with a glimpse into the rich tapestry of historical influences that have shaped the contemporary culinary landscape.

The suggestion to use a Spicy Hot Chocolate Mix in the Tiramisu recipe serves to infuse the dish with a medieval-inspired twist, infusing it with the warmth and depth of flavors that were highly valued during the medieval era. The blend of spices, such as cinnamon, long pepper, and cloves, adds an aromatic complexity to the dessert, evoking the rich and diverse flavors that were prominent in medieval cuisine. By incorporating the Spicy Hot Chocolate Mix, the recipe not only pays homage to the historical significance of spices in medieval cooking but also offers readers a unique and innovative way to experience a classic dessert through the lens of a medieval culinary narrative. This fusion of flavors creates a delightful harmony of traditional and contemporary tastes, inviting readers to embark on a culinary journey that bridges the gap between the past and the present.

Ingredients:

- 3 large egg yolks
- 1/2 cup granulated sugar
- 8 ounces mascarpone cheese
- 1/2 cup heavy cream

- 1/4 cup Spicy Chocolate Mix
- 1 cup brewed coffee, cooled
- 2 tablespoons rum or coffee liqueur
- 1 package ladyfingers (24 pieces)
- Unsweetened cocoa powder, for dusting

Instructions:

1. In a heatproof bowl, whisk together the egg yolks and granulated sugar. Place the bowl over a pan of simmering water, making sure the bottom of the bowl doesn't touch the water. Whisk constantly until the sugar has dissolved and the mixture is smooth and slightly thickened. Remove from heat and let it cool slightly.

2. In a separate bowl, whip the mascarpone cheese and heavy cream until smooth and well combined. Gently fold in the cooled egg yolk mixture and the Spicy Chocolate Mix until fully incorporated.

3. In a shallow dish, combine the brewed coffee and rum or coffee liqueur.

4. Quickly dip each ladyfinger into the coffee mixture, ensuring they are moistened but not overly saturated.

5. Arrange a layer of the soaked ladyfingers in the bottom of a serving dish.

6. Spread half of the mascarpone mixture over the ladyfingers.
7. Repeat the layers with the remaining ladyfingers and mascarpone mixture.

8. Dust the top with unsweetened cocoa powder.

9. Cover and refrigerate the tiramisu for at least 4 hours

or overnight, allowing the flavors to meld and the dessert to set.

10. Serve chilled and savor the delightful blend of rich chocolate, aromatic spices, and the smooth creaminess of the mascarpone in this luscious Spicy Medieval Hot Chocolate Flavored Tiramisu, perfect for indulging in a touch of decadence and sophistication.

This Spicy Medieval Hot Chocolate Flavored Tiramisu with Cocoa and Mascarpone offers a tantalizing twist on the classic Italian dessert, infusing it with the warm and aromatic essence of the Spicy Chocolate Mix and creating a luxurious treat that's sure to captivate your taste buds and leave you craving for more.

§

Spicy Medieval Hot Chocolate Infused Chocolate Truffles with Cocoa Powder

Chocolate truffles are a type of confectionery typically made with a rich, decadent mixture of chocolate and cream, forming a ganache center that is then coated with various ingredients such as cocoa powder, chopped nuts, or chocolate shavings. The name "truffle" comes from their physical resemblance to the prized underground fungus known as truffles. While they share a similar rounded shape with the edible fungi, chocolate truffles are not in any way related to or derived from the mushroom known as truffle.
The name "truffle" was given to these chocolate confections due to their visual resemblance to the irregular, lumpy shape of the earthy, aromatic truffle mushroom. This similarity in appearance, along with the luxurious and indulgent qualities of the chocolate treat, led to the adoption of the term "truffle" in the culinary world.

It's important to note that despite sharing the name, chocolate truffles do not contain any actual truffle mushroom. Rather, they are a delightful and decadent sweet treat enjoyed for their luxurious texture, rich chocolate flavor, and the various creative coatings that add an extra layer of taste and texture.

Chocolate truffles have become a popular delicacy appreciated by chocolate enthusiasts worldwide, admired for their smooth, melt-in-your-mouth texture and the wide array of flavor combinations and coatings that make them a versatile and indulgent dessert. Whether enjoyed on their own or as part of a dessert platter, chocolate truffles offer a delightful and luxurious experience that is distinctly separate from the culinary world of the truffle mushroom.

Ingredients:

- 8 ounces bittersweet chocolate, finely chopped
- 1/2 cup heavy cream
- 2 tablespoons unsalted butter, softened
- 1/4 cup Spicy Chocolate Mix
- 1/2 cup unsweetened cocoa powder, for coating the truffles

Instructions:

1. Place the finely chopped bittersweet chocolate in a heatproof bowl.

2. In a saucepan, heat the heavy cream over medium heat until it just begins to boil.

3. Pour the hot cream over the chopped chocolate and let it sit for 1-2 minutes. Then, stir until the chocolate is completely melted and smooth.

4. Add the softened butter and Spicy Chocolate Mix to the chocolate mixture, stirring until well combined.

5. Cover the bowl and refrigerate the mixture for at least 2 hours or until it is firm enough to handle.

6. Using a spoon or a small scoop, portion the chocolate mixture into small balls and roll them between your palms to form smooth truffles.

7. Roll each truffle in the unsweetened cocoa powder until fully coated.

8. Place the coated truffles on a parchment-lined baking sheet.

9. Refrigerate the truffles for an additional 30 minutes to set.

10. Serve the Spicy Medieval Hot Chocolate Infused Chocolate Truffles with Cocoa Powder and enjoy the luxurious blend of rich chocolate, warm spices, and the delicate bitterness of the cocoa powder in every delectable bite.

These Spicy Medieval Hot Chocolate Infused Chocolate Truffles with Cocoa Powder offer a delightful indulgence that combines the luxurious essence of smooth chocolate with the aromatic complexity of the Spicy Chocolate Mix, creating an exquisite treat that's sure to captivate your senses and leave you craving for more.

§

Spicy Medieval Hot Chocolate Infused Waffles with Whipped Cream and Chocolate Sauce

Waffles have a rich history that dates back to ancient Greece, where they were cooked between two metal plates over an open fire. Over time, waffles have evolved into the beloved breakfast and dessert item we know today. The modern waffle iron, with its familiar grid pattern, was patented in the 1860s, leading to the widespread popularity of waffles around the world.

The appeal of waffles lies in their delightful combination of crisp exterior and fluffy interior, creating a textural contrast that is both satisfying and comforting. Their versatility allows them to be enjoyed in various forms, whether sweet or savory, making them a popular choice for breakfast, brunch, and dessert.

While making waffles is generally straightforward, there are a few common pitfalls that can result in less-than-ideal outcomes. Overmixing the batter can lead to tough and dense waffles, while undermixing may result in uneven texture. Additionally, not preheating the waffle iron adequately or not greasing it properly can cause the waffles to stick and tear, making them difficult to remove from the iron.

In a medieval-themed cookbook, the inclusion of waffles can serve as a nod to the historical significance of early versions of this beloved dish. While the specific waffle as we know it today might not have existed during the medieval era, the concept of batter-based cakes cooked between hot plates has historical roots that can be traced back to ancient times. The use of ingredients and flavors that were available during the medieval period, combined with contemporary interpretations, allows for a creative exploration of how historical influences continue to shape modern culinary experiences. The presence of waffles in a medieval-themed cookbook offers readers an engaging and flavorful connection to the past while celebrating the enduring legacy of culinary traditions through the ages.

Ingredients:

For the Waffles:

- 1 3/4 cups all-purpose flour
- 1/4 cup cornstarch
- 2 tablespoons granulated sugar
- 1 tablespoon baking powder
- 1/2 teaspoon baking soda
- 1/2 teaspoon salt
- 2 cups buttermilk
- 1/2 cup vegetable oil
- 2 large eggs
- 1/4 cup Spicy Chocolate Mix
- 1 teaspoon vanilla extract

For the Whipped Cream and Chocolate Sauce:

- 1 cup heavy cream
- 2 tablespoons powdered sugar
- 1 teaspoon vanilla extract
- 1/2 cup chocolate chips
- 1/4 cup heavy cream

Instructions:

1. Preheat your waffle iron according to the manufacturer's instructions.

2. In a large bowl, whisk together the flour, cornstarch, sugar, baking powder, baking soda, and salt.

3. In a separate bowl, whisk together the buttermilk, vegetable oil, eggs, Spicy Chocolate Mix, and vanilla extract.

4. Pour the wet ingredients into the dry ingredients and mix until just combined.

5. Ladle the waffle batter into the preheated waffle iron and cook according to the manufacturer's instructions, or until the waffles are golden and crisp.

6. While the waffles are cooking, prepare the whipped cream. In a mixing bowl, beat the heavy cream, powdered sugar, and vanilla extract until stiff peaks form.

7. For the chocolate sauce, heat the chocolate chips and 1/4 cup of heavy cream in a microwave-safe bowl in 30-second intervals, stirring until smooth and well combined.

8. Serve the Spicy Medieval Hot Chocolate Infused Waffles with a dollop of whipped cream, drizzle generously with the chocolate sauce, and savor the delightful blend of warm spices, rich chocolate, and the fluffy texture of the waffles, creating a luxurious breakfast or dessert experience that's sure to leave you craving more.

Enjoy the enticing combination of rich, warm flavors and the delightful contrast of textures, inviting you to indulge in the luxurious and comforting essence of a medieval-inspired waffle feast.

§

Warm Spicy Medieval Hot Chocolate Bread Pudding with Vanilla Sauce

The use of vanilla in medieval cooking is not well-documented, as vanilla, derived from the orchid genus Vanilla, is native to Mexico and was introduced to

Europe much later. While the Aztecs are known to have used vanilla as a flavoring agent, it wasn't until the 16th century that it was introduced to Europe by Spanish conquistadors. Therefore, vanilla itself would not have been available during the medieval period in Europe.

The use of spices and flavorings was, however, a crucial aspect of medieval culinary practices. Spices such as cinnamon, nutmeg, and cloves were highly prized during this time and were used to enhance the flavors of various dishes. Their rarity and exotic nature made them a symbol of wealth and sophistication, with a significant portion of medieval trade centered around the spice route.

While the specific use of vanilla may not have been present in medieval European cuisine, the concept of incorporating exotic and aromatic flavors to enhance the taste of dishes was a prevalent practice. The introduction of vanilla to Europe in later centuries led to its integration into various culinary traditions, gradually becoming a beloved and widely used flavoring agent in European cooking.

In modern times, vanilla has become a staple in many dessert recipes and is celebrated for its rich, sweet, and floral flavor. Its addition to the Warm Spicy Medieval Hot Chocolate Bread Pudding with Vanilla Sauce offers a contemporary twist on a traditional dish, showcasing the evolution of culinary tastes and the incorporation of diverse flavors from different corners of the world.

Ingredients:

For the Bread Pudding:

- 8 cups day-old bread, cut into cubes
- 2 cups whole milk

- 1 cup heavy cream
- 1 cup Spicy Chocolate Mix
- 4 large eggs
- 1 teaspoon vanilla extract
- 1/2 cup chopped nuts (such as pecans or walnuts)

For the Vanilla Sauce:

- 1 cup whole milk
- 1 cup heavy cream
- 1/2 cup granulated sugar
- 1 vanilla bean, split lengthwise and seeds scraped out

Instructions:

1. Preheat your oven to 350°F (175°C). Grease a baking dish with butter.

2. Place the bread cubes in the prepared baking dish.

3. In a saucepan, heat the milk and heavy cream over medium heat until just simmering. Remove from heat and whisk in the Spicy Chocolate Mix until fully combined.

4. In a separate bowl, whisk together the eggs and vanilla extract. Slowly pour the chocolate mixture into the egg mixture, whisking continuously.

5. Pour the chocolate custard over the bread cubes, pressing down gently to ensure all the bread is coated. Let it sit for 15 minutes to allow the bread to soak up the custard.

6. Sprinkle the chopped nuts over the top of the bread pudding.

7. Bake for 35-40 minutes, or until the top is golden and the custard is set.

8. While the bread pudding is baking, prepare the vanilla sauce. In a saucepan, combine the milk, heavy cream, and granulated sugar. Add the vanilla bean and seeds. Heat over medium heat until the sugar has dissolved and the sauce has thickened slightly.

9. Once the bread pudding is done, let it cool for a few minutes before serving warm with the vanilla sauce drizzled over the top.

Indulge in the comforting warmth of the Warm Spicy Medieval Hot Chocolate Bread Pudding with Vanilla Sauce, savoring the rich, chocolatey flavors complemented by the aromatic essence of warm spices and the luscious sweetness of the vanilla-infused sauce.

§

Warm Spicy Medieval Hot Chocolate Custard with Caramelized Sugar Topping

Custards have a rich culinary history that can be traced back to ancient times. Their creamy, luscious texture and delicate sweetness have made them a beloved dessert around the world. While the exact origin of custards is not definitively documented, they were certainly enjoyed during the medieval period, where custards were prepared using a variety of ingredients, including milk, eggs, and sometimes honey or sugar. These custards were often flavored with spices like cinnamon, nutmeg, and cloves, which were highly prized during the medieval era and added a delightful aromatic complexity to the desserts.

In the medieval context, custards were considered a luxurious treat, often served at feasts and banquets of the aristocracy. The skillful preparation of custards required a delicate balance, as overcooking could result in a curdled texture, while undercooking could lead to a runny consistency. Common medieval cooking methods involved slow, gentle heat, such as using a hot water bath or bain-marie, to ensure the custard set properly without curdling.

To elevate the Warm Spicy Medieval Hot Chocolate Custard with Caramelized Sugar Topping, the cook may consider incorporating additional elements such as a hint of orange zest to complement the warm spices, or a touch of finely chopped toasted nuts for added texture and depth. Additionally, a splash of a fine liqueur, such as Grand Marnier or Amaretto, could infuse the custard with a sophisticated twist, enhancing the overall flavor profile and creating a more complex and indulgent dessert experience.

It's important to note that while custards are relatively simple to make, there are common pitfalls that can affect their texture and taste. Overcooking the custard at too high a temperature can result in a grainy texture, while adding eggs to hot mixtures too quickly can lead to undesirable lumps. Properly tempering the eggs and ensuring a slow, gentle cooking process are essential steps to achieving a smooth and velvety custard consistency.

By understanding the origins of custards, the delicate medieval cooking techniques, and the nuances of flavor combination, the cook can masterfully create a Warm Spicy Medieval Hot Chocolate Custard with Caramelized Sugar Topping that pays homage to the rich culinary traditions of the past while embracing contemporary culinary sensibilities.

Ingredients:

For the Custard:

- 2 cups whole milk
- 1 cup heavy cream
- 1/2 cup Spicy Chocolate Mix
- 4 large eggs
- 1/2 cup granulated sugar
- 1 teaspoon vanilla extract
- Pinch of salt

For the Caramelized Sugar Topping:

- 1/2 cup granulated sugar
- 2 tablespoons water

Instructions:

1. Preheat your oven to 325°F (160°C). Place six ramekins in a large baking dish.

2. In a saucepan, heat the milk and heavy cream over medium heat until just simmering. Remove from heat and whisk in the Spicy Chocolate Mix until fully combined.

3. In a mixing bowl, whisk together the eggs, granulated sugar, vanilla extract, and a pinch of salt. Slowly pour the chocolate mixture into the egg mixture, whisking continuously.

4. Divide the custard mixture among the ramekins. Pour hot water into the baking dish, about halfway up the sides of the ramekins, creating a water bath.

5. Carefully transfer the baking dish to the preheated

oven and bake for 30-35 minutes, or until the custards are set around the edges but still slightly wobbly in the center.

6. Remove the custards from the water bath and let them cool to room temperature. Then, refrigerate for at least 2 hours or until thoroughly chilled.

7. Just before serving, make the caramelized sugar topping. In a small saucepan, combine the granulated sugar and water. Cook over medium heat, swirling the pan occasionally, until the sugar turns a deep amber color.

8. Working quickly, drizzle the caramelized sugar over each custard, allowing it to harden into a crispy topping.

9. Serve the Warm Spicy Medieval Hot Chocolate Custard with Caramelized Sugar Topping, relishing the delightful contrast between the rich, spiced custard and the crisp sweetness of the caramelized sugar, creating a luxurious dessert experience that is both comforting and indulgent.

§

Cinnamon and Long Pepper Spiced Hot Chocolate Oat Bars with Chocolate Drizzle

During the medieval period, the use of various ingredients, including rose petals, hazelnuts, and ginger, was prevalent in culinary practices. These ingredients were valued not only for their distinct flavors but also for their medicinal and aromatic properties.

Rose petals, known for their delicate floral fragrance, were often used to add a subtle perfume to dishes and were prized for their decorative appeal, especially in elaborate feasts and banquets hosted by the nobility. They were sometimes used to infuse desserts and beverages, offering a touch of elegance and sophistication to the dining experience.

Hazelnuts, with their rich, nutty flavor and satisfying crunch, were commonly used in both sweet and savory dishes during the medieval era. They were a staple in various desserts, such as cakes, pastries, and confections, and were also used to add texture and depth to meat dishes and stews. Hazelnuts were highly prized for their versatility and nutritional value, making them a sought-after ingredient in medieval cuisine.

Ginger, valued for its pungent and spicy aroma, was a popular spice in medieval cooking. It was used not only for its distinctive flavor but also for its medicinal properties, as it was believed to aid digestion and alleviate various ailments. Ginger was often incorporated into both sweet and savory dishes, adding a warm, zesty kick to everything from baked goods to meat-based preparations.

In the context of a medieval-themed cookbook, the inclusion of rose petals, hazelnuts, and ginger in the Cinnamon and Long Pepper Spiced Hot Chocolate Oat Bars with Chocolate Drizzle pays homage to the culinary traditions of the era, highlighting the use of diverse and exotic ingredients that were prized for their unique flavors and contributions to both the taste and aesthetics of medieval dishes.

The culinary technique of drizzling, particularly in the context of medieval Europe, was closely tied to the preparation and presentation of various dishes. While the precise origins of the drizzling technique are not extensively documented, the use of this method was intricately linked to the art of decorative food presentation and the enhancement of visual appeal.

During the medieval period, drizzling was often employed to add a finishing touch to desserts, pastries, and even certain meat dishes. Drizzling sauces, glazes, or melted ingredients over a dish not only imparted an additional layer of flavor but also contributed to the overall visual aesthetics, creating an alluring and appetizing appearance.

In medieval European culinary practices, the art of drizzling was considered a skill that required precision and finesse. It was often used to create intricate patterns or designs, showcasing the culinary expertise of the cook or chef. Various ingredients were utilized for drizzling, including melted chocolate, honey, fruit coulis, and flavored syrups, which were delicately applied to enhance the taste and presentation of the dish.

In the case of the Cinnamon and Long Pepper Spiced Hot Chocolate Oat Bars with Chocolate Drizzle, the application of the chocolate drizzle serves to elevate the dessert's visual appeal while imparting a decadent and indulgent finish. The drizzle not only adds a contrasting texture to the oat bars but also creates an enticing presentation that tantalizes the senses and invites the consumer to savor the rich, velvety sweetness of the chocolate. The incorporation of the drizzling technique in this recipe exemplifies the timeless culinary artistry that has transcended centuries, showcasing the enduring influence of medieval culinary practices in modern gastronomy.

By incorporating these ingredients into modern recipes, the cookbook aims to offer readers a sensory journey that celebrates the rich tapestry of historical culinary influences while infusing contemporary creativity and flavors into the culinary experience. Enjoy the delightful blend of warm spices, hearty oats, and the unexpected combination of candied ginger, roasted hazelnuts, and dried edible rose petals, all complemented by the decadent chocolate drizzle, creating a unique and flavorful treat that's sure to captivate your taste buds.

Ingredients:

For the Oat Bars:

- 1 1/2 cups old-fashioned oats
- 1 cup all-purpose flour
- 1/2 cup Spicy Chocolate Mix
- 1/2 teaspoon baking powder
- 1/4 teaspoon baking soda
- 1/4 teaspoon salt
- 1/2 cup unsalted butter, melted
- 1/3 cup honey
- 1/4 cup unsweetened applesauce
- 1 large egg
- 1 teaspoon vanilla extract
- 1/4 cup chopped candied ginger
- 1/4 cup chopped roasted hazelnuts
- 1/4 cup dried edible rose petals

For the Chocolate Drizzle:

- 1/2 cup semisweet chocolate chips
- 1 tablespoon unsalted butter

Instructions:

1. Preheat your oven to 350°F (175°C). Line an 8-inch square baking dish with parchment paper, leaving an overhang on the sides for easy removal.

2. In a large bowl, combine the oats, flour, Spicy Chocolate Mix, baking powder, baking soda, and salt.

3. In another bowl, whisk together the melted butter, honey, applesauce, egg, and vanilla extract.

4. Add the wet ingredients to the dry ingredients and mix until well combined.
5. Fold in the chopped candied ginger, roasted hazelnuts, and dried edible rose petals.

6. Press the mixture firmly and evenly into the prepared baking dish.

7. Bake for 25-30 minutes, or until the oat bars are golden and set.
8. While the oat bars are cooling, make the chocolate drizzle. In a microwave-safe bowl, heat the chocolate chips and butter in 30-second intervals, stirring until smooth and well combined.

9. Once the oat bars have cooled slightly, drizzle the chocolate mixture over the top.

10. Allow the bars to cool completely before cutting into squares and serving.

Spicy Hot Chocolate Popsicles with Cinnamon and Clove

Ingredients:

- 1 ½ cups whole milk
- 1 cup heavy cream
- ½ cup spicy hot chocolate mix
- 1 cinnamon stick
- 3 whole cloves
- Popsicle molds
- Popsicle sticks

Instructions:

1. In a saucepan over medium heat, combine the whole milk, heavy cream, spicy hot chocolate mix, cinnamon stick, and whole cloves. Stir until the mixture is well combined and the chocolate mix is fully dissolved.

2. Bring the mixture to a gentle simmer, then remove the saucepan from the heat and let it cool slightly.

3. Strain the mixture to remove the cinnamon stick and cloves, ensuring a smooth consistency.

4. Pour the mixture into popsicle molds, leaving a little space at the top for expansion.

5. Place the popsicle sticks into the molds, ensuring they are centered.

6. Freeze the popsicles for at least 6 hours or until fully set.

7. To remove the popsicles from the molds, run the molds under warm water for a few seconds. Enjoy your

spicy hot chocolate popsicles with the aromatic flavors of cinnamon and clove!

These spicy hot chocolate popsicles with the added warmth of cinnamon and clove are perfect for enjoying during warmer weather or as a delightful treat any time of the year.

§

Spicy Medieval Hot Chocolate Bread Pudding with Rum Sauce

Imagine a dessert that embodies the essence of the medieval era, a time of rich flavors and indulgent comfort. The Spicy Medieval Hot Chocolate Bread Pudding with Rum Sauce is a delightful creation that marries the robust warmth of the spicy mix with the decadent allure of the luscious rum sauce.

As this bread pudding bakes, your kitchen is enveloped in the enticing aroma of dark chocolate and fragrant spices, reminiscent of bustling medieval markets. The bread absorbs the creamy mixture, creating a sumptuously soft and moist interior while forming a golden crust that hints at the delightful textures within.

Each spoonful offers a delightful contrast between the slightly spicy undertones of the medieval hot chocolate and the sweet, velvety essence of the rum sauce, culminating in a harmonious blend that dances on your palate. The soft crunch of the nuts, if added, provides a satisfying textural element that elevates each bite, adding a delightful surprise to the overall experience.

Serve this delectable dessert warm, allowing the flavors

to unfold and the senses to revel in the richness that the medieval era has to offer. Whether enjoyed as the perfect ending to a feast or as a comforting treat on a cozy evening, this Spicy Medieval Hot Chocolate Bread Pudding with Rum Sauce is sure to transport you to a time of opulence and indulgence, leaving you with a lasting impression of the delights of the past.

Ingredients:

Spicy Medieval Hot Chocolate Bread Pudding:

- 6 cups day-old bread, cut into cubes
- 2 cups whole milk
- 1 cup heavy cream
- 1 cup spicy medieval hot chocolate mix
- 4 large eggs
- 1/2 cup granulated sugar
- 1 teaspoon vanilla extract
- 1/2 cup chopped dark chocolate
- 1/2 cup chopped nuts (optional)
- Butter for greasing

Rum Sauce:

- 1/2 cup unsalted butter
- 1/2 cup brown sugar
- 1/4 cup heavy cream
- 2 tablespoons dark rum

Instructions:

1. Preheat your oven to 350°F (175°C). Grease a 9x13 inch baking dish with butter.
2. In a large bowl, combine the bread cubes, milk, and heavy cream. Let the bread soak up the liquid for about 10 minutes.
3. In another bowl, whisk together the spicy medieval

hot chocolate mix, eggs, sugar, and vanilla extract. Pour this mixture over the soaked bread and mix well. Fold in the chopped dark chocolate and nuts if desired.

4. Pour the bread mixture into the prepared baking dish, spreading it evenly.

5. Bake for 45-50 minutes, or until the top is golden brown and the pudding is set.

6. While the bread pudding is baking, prepare the rum sauce. In a saucepan over medium heat, melt the butter. Stir in the brown sugar and cook for 2 minutes. Add the heavy cream and cook for an additional 2 minutes. Remove from heat and stir in the dark rum.

7. Serve the warm bread pudding with the rum sauce drizzled over the top. Enjoy the delicious blend of spicy medieval hot chocolate flavors and the rich, buttery rum sauce!

Fare Well

In the final pages of our culinary journey through the rich tapestry of medieval flavors, we have delved into the intricate world of both spicy and non-spicy medieval hot chocolate mixes, discovering their transformative potential in a myriad of contemporary comfort foods and desserts. We've witnessed how the warm embrace of aromatic spices and the luxurious essence of chocolate can transcend time, infusing our modern palate with a taste of history.

As we bid adieu to the ancient kitchens of the past, let us not forget that our exploration is merely the beginning of a much larger conversation. The dialogue between historic techniques and ingredients and their integration into modern culinary practices continues to unfold, inviting us to embark on an endless quest of flavor discovery and innovation.

Through this exploration, we have not only celebrated the culinary heritage of our ancestors but also paved the way for a new era of gastronomic creativity. We encourage you, dear readers, to continue this journey, to experiment fearlessly with the fusion of the old and the new, and to savor each dish as a testament to the timeless connection between tradition and innovation.

May your kitchens be filled with the spirit of the past and the promise of the future, as we continue to weave the intricate tapestry of flavors, techniques, and ingredients, honoring the legacy of our culinary history while embracing the boundless possibilities of the culinary world that awaits us. Cheers to the joy of discovery and the endless pursuit of delectable delights!

Time's Fare

In the ancient hearths where embers softly glow,
The spirit of olden cookery does still bestow,
A tale of flavors woven through time's gentle sway,
A legacy of tastes that forever shall stay.

Spices and herbs in a dance of delight,
Cinnamon, clove, and pepper unite,
In pots and pans, the alchemy begins,
Where history and modernity gracefully spins.

From the cauldrons of old to the stoves of today,
The essence of tradition forever holds sway,
As chocolate and warmth blend in sweet harmony,
A tapestry of flavors, a timeless culinary symphony.

In the heart of each dish, a tale does unfold,
Of medieval feasts, both humble and bold,
Where the past meets the present, a culinary embrace,
Awakening our senses, transporting us to a timeless
place.

Let us honor the past while embracing the new,
A culinary journey, both vibrant and true,
May the flavors of yore and the tastes of today,
Guide us on a path where creativity holds sway.

So let us raise our ladles and toast to the feast,
Where tradition and innovation forever shall meet,
In the kitchen's embrace, where history does play,
We celebrate the spirit of cookery, both then and today.

Recipes for the Chocolate Mixes

While not the exact recipes for the Walker & Mason mixes, the following formulas will do in a pinch. Enjoy!

Medieval Hot Chocolate Mix

Ingredients:
1 cup cocoa powder
1 cup granulated sugar
1 teaspoon ground cinnamon
1/2 teaspoon ground nutmeg
1/4 teaspoon ground cloves
Pinch of salt

Spicy Medieval Hot Chocolate Mix

Ingredients:
1 cup unsweetened cocoa powder
1 cup granulated sugar
1 teaspoon ground cinnamon
2 teaspoons ground long pepper
1/2 teaspoon ground Guajillo chili
1/4 teaspoon ground nutmeg
Pinch of ground cloves

www.ingramcontent.com/pod-product-compliance
Lightning Source LLC
Chambersburg PA
CBHW051317120626
46547CB00015B/2274